Transcending the White Picket Fence

Transcending the White Picket Fence

A Modern Woman's Guide to Wealth, Abundance and Freedom

Jasmine Marra

Published by Game Changer Publishing

Paperback ISBN: 978-1-966659-34-1

Hardcover ISBN: 978-1-966659-35-8

Digital ISBN: 978-1-966659-36-5

GAME CHANGER
PUBLISHING
www.GameChangerPublishing.com

Dedication

To my incredible husband, Chris. Your unwavering support, love, and belief in me have been my foundation. Thank you for walking this journey with me and for always cheering me on. It has been the greatest blessing of my life to build my life with you.

To my three beautiful children, Rowan, Lucca, and Matteo You are my greatest inspirations and the light of my life. May this book serve as a reminder that anything is possible with passion, purpose, and love.

Acknowledgments

To Dad, Mom, Alicia + Nathan - I'm not sure how we got so lucky to call each other family, but I am grateful that no matter how far - I deeply know we have each other.

To John + Josephine - I am in deep gratitude to be able to call you both my inlaws. Thank you for being the best Nonno and Nonna to our children and reminding us that family always comes first.

To Jess - who not only captured the most beautiful picture for the cover of this book but who has walked each step in transcending my white picket fence with me. Thank you for wiping my tears, allowing me to be me, and loving me through each stage.

To Lori - who is my business wingwoman - spiraling higher while staying grounded in laughter and fun as a women leader is the best with you by my side.

To Sam - since the moment we met at Lady Dunn, you have been my friend through thick and thin. I am in deep gratitude for your enduring friendship.

To Jasmine - I finally found another friend named Jasmine (yay) - thank you for always showing up to capture my family and me in the most beautiful photos - including for this book!

To Meg - you made me believe in friendship at first connection over the internet. Thank you for becoming my business bestie and turning our collective dreams into reality together with the creation of amazingly transformative programs like Wealth Alchemy and Flow.

To Tanya, the OG friend - there are days when I still ache for an apple cider and drive to the beach. I'm grateful our friendship no matter how far.

With Love + Abundance Always
—Jasmine xo (aka Catalina, Mom and Bestie!)

Read This First

Just to say thanks for buying and reading my book,
I would like to invite you into my FREE Facebook Group
called Quantum Femme Wealth: Joyful First Generation
Millionaire Money Talk! No Strings attached!

Transcending the White Picket Fence

A MODERN WOMAN'S GUIDE TO WEALTH, ABUNDANCE AND FREEDOM

JASMINE MARRA

Foreword

Your brain, body, and what was passed down from generation to generation in your family is a part of everything you do, including how you handle and treat your money. These core pieces have everything to do with your relationships with food, others, money, and any of your day-to-day activities. The intertwined reality of what has been, is being, and what will manifest in your current reality to create what you believe you are designed to have and hold.

From my experience in working with hundreds of clients on their marketing and sales approach and my own untangling of my relationship with money, it is very clear to me that when you upgrade your beliefs around money, money starts working for you. When you continue to follow the same programming that led you to open this book (which you won't after reading it), money will continue to feel like a distant cousin that you see once every ten years.

Inconsistent income was a part of my own story for a very long time. As much as I worked on my strategies and money mindset, it was as if I put a gate up at times and didn't want to allow any more in. It was in a period of expansion and taking up more space (aka allowing more money in) that Jasmine and I met in a rather unconventional way. I had happened upon jasmine's Instagram profile several months before, and we had shared a few words back and forth. Then, she posted more about her story, and I was FLOORED. Our stories were so incredibly similar, and yet this woman was a multi-millionaire! It was as if in that moment, she gave me permission to let go of the trauma that haunted me from previous financial abuse. We got on a Zoom call together and were immediately sisters. I couldn't believe she wanted to partner with me. Who was I to have a business partner of such high caliber?! Jasmine Marra is MEDICINE. Her joy is infectious and a true representation of wealth on all levels.

Transcending the White Picket Fence is your guide to optimizing both the internal and external programs that impact your financial dynamics to help you reach your goals. This book is based on science, energetics, and speaks with so much love and wisdom. Jasmine unravels the mystery of becoming wealthy in such a personal way that you will feel like you are just sitting across from her, having a warm cup of coffee and chit-chatting. She embodies wealth at all levels and will have you believing that you, too, can achieve anything you put your mind to.

Even though I have done extensive work on my relationship with money—learning how to make it work for me rather than the other way around—this book has further enhanced my ability to identify constraints that are preventing my finances from flowing at increasingly higher levels. It has helped me to connect more of my own unwise choices with money in order to create a firmer foundation for my life, my family, and my business.

Almost every single person has some form of money-related trauma. Remember that trauma is simply an overwhelming experience that triggers an emotional response from you. This could be a feeling of excitement, nervousness, fear, or any other emotion that is not at baseline for the human brain (aka a regulated nervous system). Cleaning out these experiences that have become part of the brain and nervous system can be incredibly healing. Of course, engaging in healthy relationships is a large part of creating a healthy relationship with money as well to create a nervous system that can value money without unhealthy attachments. In addition, your relationship with yourself is a top priority. Jasmine dives into this topic by teaching us the "Wealthy Woman Belief Codes," which can take you on a personal journey of self-development leading to financial development should you choose to incorporate them into your programming. My suggestion is that you do.

My hope is that, like me, you will develop a "Millionaire Mindset" through reading this book and decide that you are fully capable of reaching your financial goals—whatever they may be. When I look back on my own money story, it is clear that my nervous system was at "energetic set points" during my own growth as a successful entrepreneur. Even though I had done extensive money work and returned to school to receive a Masters in Business Administration, finances still felt funky to me. When I reached my first $20.000 month, I was overjoyed! I allowed myself to move into the house of my dreams, with the partner of my dreams. But when, the next month, I only had a $5k month, my nervous system went haywire.

Part of this was my generational money story and past abuse.

Part of this was my energetic set point.

Part of this was not understanding the physical aspect of money or how to handle it.

Jasmine Marra ties each of these pieces together beautifully so that when YOU receive that amount you never could have imagined… you'll know exactly what to do to keep it flowing in saving you guesswork and time and offering a shortcut to developing a healthier view on money. I hope you will enjoy reading this book as much as I did and make the decision to alchemize your finances, allowing a gateway to becoming the first generational joyful millionaire in your family!

—*Meg (Edelen) Zeek, MBA*
    CEO Abundance Uprising
    Transformational Leadership + Business Facilitator

Introduction

I grew up in a loving household that taught me to get a good job, marry a nice guy, be a good girl, and save for retirement. We were a family of five living in a small town on the east coast of Canada. I was the oldest child of three, which meant I got to blaze the way forward and hold the responsibility of always being the example—aka double down on the guidelines of life listed above. As a family, we rarely went out to eat, always opting for a home-cooked meal, and while many others had designer clothes, I most certainly did not. It was Walmart brand all the way for this girl—which, in truth, was just fine with me. It was a good life that taught me to be realistic, value family, focus on security, and never, ever go into debt. My dad was a teacher, and my mom worked at the hospital. More than anything, I wanted to make them proud. So I went about my life doing the things I was taught were the "right" way so I could meet the expectations of the world and succeed in life. I went to school and got straight A's. I attended post-secondary education and obtained an undergraduate degree in Marketing and International Business, and to seal the deal, I also earned my master's in Business Administration. I didn't want to leave any stone unturned and had to make sure I was extra qualified.

Now, onto the relationship department. I met and married a nice guy. I landed the perfect government job with a pension and started a little family, welcoming my first baby boy. This was it—my white picket fence at last! I had arrived, and received much love, validation, and appreciation for where I was. I had made my parents and society proud. And while I had checked all the boxes, there was a tiny feeling of unhappiness deep inside. That little nagging feeling—you know the one—that tiny question of doubt inside: *Is this what life is really all about?*

I managed to find "comfortable societal happiness" on this journey and ignored that little feeling inside until, in 2014, my world was rocked in a way I never could have imagined. My white-picket life started to unravel at the seams, and suddenly, all the things I had strived for—being a good girl, marrying the nice guy, and never going into debt—blew up in my face. In what felt like an instant, I lost my job and, consequently, my coveted pension. My financial situation became so strained it made me lose sleep. I had no idea what I was doing as a first-time mom, and my marriage, no matter how hard I tried, was slowly falling apart one day at a time.

Before I share what happened next, I need you to appreciate how awful this was for me. Everything—and I mean *everything*—that I feared was now on my doorstep. This was not supposed to happen. I had spent my entire life up to that point trying to avoid every single thing I was now about to face, and it made me paralyzed with fear and sick to my stomach at the same time. I was at a complete loss. Everything I believed to be true was no longer so. Everything I thought I had to do to achieve happiness, wealth, and freedom was in question. And I was deeply terrified—bone-shaking, insomnia-inducing terrified—and absolutely frozen in place, like a baby deer caught in headlights on a dark night. I didn't even know how to take a step forward, let alone which step to take.

Before I knew it, I found myself a single mom, selling my marital home, in the midst of a separation, and in proverbial debt. In the blink of an eye, I went from the seemingly perfect picture of white-picket-fence happiness to an unemployed, divorced, single mom with over $50,000 in debt. Have you ever seen that moment in *Eat Pray Love* where she's sitting in the bathroom crying and praying because she has nowhere else to turn? Yeah, I could have written that scene as I lived it in real life. I was an absolute hot anxiety mess and had no idea what to do next or where to turn. I didn't even know who I was anymore. My previous identity had unraveled as fast as you could microwave a pizza pocket. I was questioning the very foundation of everything I had previously known to be true. What did true happiness really mean? Was the white-picket-fence mentality real? Was job security even a thing? What did it mean to be wealthy? To be free? And most of all, *How in the name of Smokey Bear on a shrimp cracker did I get here?*

They say there are defining moments in our lives. For me, this was my defining moment. Truly, there is my life before this moment and my life after. The universe was forcing me to re-examine my life with a swift kick in the booty. And as with any material growth, it was deeply, deeply uncomfortable. Yet, it was this very difficult moment in my life that created the opportunity for me to examine in great detail: Who was I, actually? What made me happy? What made me feel free? Why did I always do things for others rather than for myself? And this thing we call money—why was I giving up so much energy and gosh-forsaken time for it?

Because of this defining moment in my life, I finally gave myself the grace and space to define a new way forward. One that no longer just accepted what I was told was "the right thing to do" but instead was intentional about exploring what brought me wealth, abundance, and freedom. My experiences showed me that I could no longer accept the things I had learned about money, freedom, and happiness through society and others. I now knew that this way of life definitely did not work for me. My world unraveling left no shadow of a doubt that it was time to march to the beat of my own drum. There had to be a better way, and I was determined to find it.

And things were different for me in this moment—I was a mom now, and I had a son to care for on my own. Looking into his young eyes, I knew I had to change this—for him, for myself, and for the world. Deep down, I just knew that there had to be another way to live life. This moment sent me on the most magical journey of rewiring my ingrained beliefs, stepping into a new Wealthy Woman identity, and exploring what it means to be truly wealthy, financially free, happy, and joyful in every sense of the word—to rediscover who I was, in the essence of my being.

Looking back, what happened next can only be described as a true quantum leap, and I don't use that word in a colloquial sense. This experience was more aligned with the scientific definition. In this sense, a quantum leap refers to a sudden and significant change or advancement, which makes limited sense in the space and time provided. In a scientific context, quantum leaps describe the transition of an electron between energy levels in an atom, which is a discrete and significant shift. This is exactly what happened to me.

I shifted from being a single mom with $50,000 in debt to being happily remarried to my soulmate and a self-made millionaire in less than five years. And no, I didn't just meet and marry a millionaire guy (though he is one in a million). In fact, he was divorced too, and was working to clean up his own financial health following that experience. Rather, this is a journey of self-discovery and a redefinition of wealth, both energetically and physically, as a divine and infinite woman reaching deep into the core of potentiality. I know, I know—it sounds impossible. But I assure you, on all that is sacred, it's true, and I am writing this book so you can apply what I learned and do this too!

In the falling away of my old identity, I slowly found the power within to allow myself to rediscover what wealth, freedom, and abundance were all about. I came to understand that the essence of who we are as humans doesn't change with external things like more money or accomplishments. I gave myself the space to rediscover what it means to be truly wealthy, and reconnected with the internal source found deep inside myself. I sought healers, therapists, and counselors, and spent hundreds and thousands of hours studying, reflecting, receiving coaching, meditating, and visualizing. I read, ate, and breathed, becoming a new version of myself. I gave myself the opportunity to explore who I was again, no longer operating under the old conscious and unconscious beliefs I held. I was vibrantly alive and abundant in every respect—from personal joy to an overflowing bank account.

I studied lack and abundance. I activated curiosity, put myself in circles I'd never been in before, and took an executive job in finance. I tried new things and gave myself the space to explore a new identity. I shifted my reality so fast it would make your head spin—and I did it in a way that felt really, really darn good. It felt aligned, elevated, and exploratory. I discovered a transcended version of myself that left behind all expectations of others and stepped into my own infinite personal power—a rock-solid newfound core. I finally discovered the power to lead myself—not to seek validation but to turn inward to my own inner knowing with trust and connection. And I know deep down, if more people had the knowledge I gained along my journey, they too could live a truly wealthy, abundant, liberated life.

I feel a purpose-filled calling to support women just like you in transforming your relationship with financial freedom and money, and in building intergenerational wealth. To say goodbye to hustle, grind, and unhappiness and hello to true financial freedom, abundance, joy, gratitude, and wealth. To normalize wealth in the hands of women and create a community of money matriarchs who know that their value as humans is separate from the balance in their bank account—and who no longer allow money to be a restriction on what is possible. To shift the paradigm for women like us—finding joy in the simple moments of abundance and moving away from the external race for riches— toward a focus on inner happiness and joy sourced from within, which radiates outward into external manifestations. In this paradigm, money becomes simply a tool to fulfill the highest purpose and deepest desires.

I transitioned from playing small and safe, trying to keep things secure, to elevating my happiness, expanding my mind exponentially, overflowing my bank account, and inspiring thousands of other women to do the same.

Through this journey, I realized that women are simply not taught about money, prioritizing themselves, or their happiness.

According to the Wealth Equity Index by WTW, in collaboration with the World Economic Forum, women on average, accumulate only 74% of the wealth that men do at retirement. This disparity is driven by factors such as gender pay gaps, delayed career trajectories, and caregiving responsibilities, which disproportionately affect women's ability to build wealth. Further, it was only in 1974 that women in the U.S. gained the right to open a credit card under their own name without the signature of a man. We, as women, are undoubtedly making up for lost time. And yet—as women—we are so hard on ourselves when we feel uncomfortable about money or don't know where to turn.

I deeply believe that, as a society, we need to shift this.

And if we're going to shift it, we have to start by dismantling the common societal messages that women constantly receive about money—things like, "Nice girls don't talk about money," or "Money is a male matter," or "Don't worry your pretty head over that." To this, I say a hard no. I have a deep-seated belief that money in the hands of conscious women will change the world. And as a result, as women, as a sisterhood, we need to talk about it more. We need to create safe spaces to talk about money, how it makes us feel, and how to learn more about it.

So let's talk about money. Let's talk about wealth, joy, abundance, and happiness. Let's get our hands dirty in everything we're not "supposed" to so we can change the fabric of what it means to be Wealthy Women. This book aims to start the conversation, to allow us to address the pain points of how we feel about money as women, and to challenge what we believe we can and can't do. It's about overcoming fear-based, self-limiting beliefs as we aim to blaze a trail for generations of women following in our footsteps. Not just through the physical passing of money, but through a profound shift in mindset—a sisterhood of women intergenerationally healing our relationship with money. This allows us to raise our collective abundance consciousness and rediscover a deep love for our lives. It's about stepping off the oppressive hamster wheel and transcending the white-picket-fence mentality, embracing the infinite possibilities available to you today as a modern woman.

This book will show you how to calculate your net worth so you understand where you're at today and help you discover where you need to go. It will help you explore your generational money beliefs, identify any money blocks you might have, and dissolve them to allow more money to flow in. It will also demystify manifestation by explaining the science behind why your belief system matters and share **Wealthy Woman Belief Codes** to help shortcut your path to financial freedom. This book will encourage you to contemplate your ultimate lifestyle so that, when you fall in love with your life again, you are clear on what you want to design with the money that flows in. It will guide you in determining joyful income generators that will allow you to build your wealth intentionally. Lastly, I hope it will help you become brave—brave enough to expand into a new reality, take action, regulate your nervous system, and prepare your body for the new wealthy reality that is your divine birthright.

This book is for any woman who dreams of becoming the first joyful millionaire in her family. A woman who is ready to take action, embrace change, expand, and put growth first. A woman who is bold, ready to take risks, and lead herself into a new reality of potential financial freedom, joy, and gratitude. You're a trailblazer who knows deep down that you're meant for more—a woman who wants to define what "having it all" truly means for herself. You want your relationship with money to feel easy, fun, and fulfilling. You're ready to be the CEO of your own money and destiny, and you want to start a movement to normalize wealth in the hands of women. You're ready to open your heart to new ideas, new realities, and to bring forth your deepest desires. If you resonate with any of this, I am deeply grateful that you have this book in your Wealthy Woman hands.

There are four key things you need to quantum leap your life into its most abundant, wealthy state:

1. An open mind and willingness to activate new ideas.
2. A focused commitment to your new wealth approach.
3. Clarity of purpose and your *why*.
4. The guts to take action.

You simply cannot quantum leap your wealth, happiness, and freedom to the next level without these elements together.

My dream for you is that this book illuminates a path forward for you to become financially free, abundant, joyful, and the first female millionaire in your family. I want to get you excited about the possibilities that exist uniquely for you. To know deeply in your soul that it doesn't matter your circumstances, where you were born, who you are today, when you last believed in yourself, or what you're struggling with—even your current financial situation. Whatever the case, you have the limitless potential to shift into exponential happiness and wealth.

This book is about saying goodbye to traditional advice and embracing a new way forward to financial freedom for women. We are up against a specific societal program that prevents us from becoming as financially free as we can be. I will introduce some new ideas, which I call "Wealthy Woman Codes," on how to not just build more money and income, but actually create generational wealth that can change the financial fabric for generations to come—joyfully and abundantly. I hope this book provides you with practical applications to identify and address your money blocks, challenge conventional wisdom, and inspire you to think of new ways to generate income, build wealth, and contemplate your deepest desires for life alignment. I want to help you unlock the unique insights within your heart and bring them into reality without having to worry about money as a constraint. If you've picked up this book, it is no accident. The information in this book is meant for you—becoming a first-generation millionaire is already within your realm of potential. By picking up this book, you're signaling to the universe that you desire more and that you're ready to do the work to shift your reality to new heights.

As you read this introduction, there is one last thing I need you to know: This is not just a book you just read or leave on your nightstand. It is a gateway for you, designed to transform you—but you must actively step inside. It means engaging your activation energy. As many personal development enthusiasts understand, consuming content is only one piece of the puzzle. I don't want this to be just another book you read; I want it to be an opportunity for you to grasp true wealth in your life. Give yourself the sacred space to contemplate these ideas and concepts, integrate them, and make a change. Try new things to see what feels right, and identify areas where you need to grow and expand. Contemplate, integrate, implement, and activate. I have designed this book with activation in mind. Each chapter includes reflection questions and activations that are meant to help you call in the highest, wealthiest version of yourself. While engaging your activation energy might take longer, I promise this is a necessary step to call in new quantum abundance in your life. I am deeply grateful to share my innermost thoughts about wealth and happiness with you. I hope this book illuminates a way forward for you to transcend the typical white-picket-fence dream and quantum leap into becoming the first joyful generational female millionaire in your family.

Before we dive into this journey together, you might be wondering why you should listen to me. Beyond having shifted my own reality from an unhappy single mom with $50,000 in debt to a happily married mom of three and a multi-millionaire, I am also the owner of a real estate investment company and the founder of a women's coaching company called Quantum Femme Wealth. I have an MBA, and I had a successful 20-year career as a marketing professional, seven of those years at the executive table of a financial firm assisting clients with debt restructuring. Not only do I have practical experience in building my own businesses and shifting my reality, but I have also helped empower many women to achieve financial freedom, joy, and happiness.

I've helped thousands of women just like you transform their wealth and happiness into a new reality, but you don't have to take my word for it. Here's what some of my clients had to say:

"The 1:1 coaching I've received with Jasmine has been invaluable. She's helping me become the mother, wife, and boss that I wanted to be. Even though I've run a business for five years, I'm finally starting to realize what it actually means to be a happy, healthy, financially free woman and

entrepreneur. Because of that, I'm now making decisions in my business to align with my true dream life. I can see an easy roadmap forward."
–Jennifer,
Owner Calgary Institute of Counselling, Canada

"I am so grateful for all the support, encouragement and expert guidance I have received through the Wealth Alchemy group program. I knew that I had some heavy work to do around money mindset, but I didn't realize how deeply it was impacting me. Through the loving guidance I received, I have broken through one of my biggest barriers to money and allow myself to receive in all forms. I can't tell you how much lighter I feel."
–Melissia Melendez
Transformational Leadership Coach, USA

"1:1 Coaching with Jasmine has truly transformed my financial outlook. Not only do I now have a plan to pay down debt, but I have also done a 180 degree with my spending and overgiving. Encouraging me to do the things I was avoiding in my finances has been the gateway to freedom. I am also about to purchase my first 4-plex to 10x my business and build a legacy of impact! I cannot recommend working with Jasmine enough. It has been the best thing I have done for my mindset, wealth and life in years!"
–Nadine,
Canada

"The Wealth Alchemy group program with Jasmine + Meg has been a life-changing experience. The sisterhood created is like having a personal cheer-leading squad through every shift and breakthrough… exploring the roots of my money mindset was truly eye-opening… it feels like a massive weight has been lifted, and now I can finally move forward with a millionaire mindset, and a renewed sense of freedom and abundance."
–Courtney Christine,
Boss Goddess Self-Love and Intimacy Coach

"Jasmine helped me realize a significant limiting belief. I believed that more money equals more burnout, which has been a major roadblock in achieving

greater abundance for myself. Also, doing the life-alignment exercise made me really think about what I do for my future, as I feel like I didn't have a super clear picture of my goals since COVID."
–Samantha,
Owner Samantha Nicole Esthetics, Canada

"Jasmine encouraged me to take my power back and that I held the reins to my own life. Wealth is way more than just money. Wealth is fulfillment in your life as a whole. She gave me the keys to open the doors to the various possibilities in my life that I hadn't considered or was too scared to step through."
–Stephanie,
Owner Choose YOU First, Empowerment + Relationship Coach

As you read this book, my hope for you is that it plants a seed of wealthy possibility—that you believe in yourself and your future, your happiness, and your potential for financial freedom as much as I do for you. I believe, at the core of my soul, that we are all placed here with divine downloads we are called to live out, and that each of us is blessed with the opportunity to create a life that is fulfilled and meaningful by our own definition. I believe that money is simply an energetic exchange; a tool to create value for each other and to build a life we love, allowing us to play by our own rules and elevate to new heights as women.

My hope is that you feel empowered as a woman to become the first millionaire in your family—in a happy, aligned, and healthy way. See this book as a gateway, an opportunity to build a new life exactly as you desire. Explore the ideas, activate them, and keep what works for you as you navigate a path forward for yourself and for the generations to come. You go first, for all women.

In Abundance Always,

—Jasmine xo

CHAPTER 1

What in the Madonna is a Millionaire?

"Stop buying things you don't need to impress people you don't even like."
–Suze Orman

O kay, before we dig into the millionaire stuff, you might be curious to know a little more about me. I'd describe myself as a badass working mom of three with a tank of resilience that would put a marathon runner to shame. Most days, I kick my days off with protein shakes and passion, driven to make a difference in the world with my family. Becoming a mother changed a lot for me—it carved out a whole new perspective and appreciation for life.

I have 20 years of marketing experience, with seven of those years spent sitting at the executive table of a financial firm before I decided to dive into the world of wealth generation for women. I grew up in a small town in Canada, raised by two wonderful parents, alongside my brother and sister. I have fond memories of my sister and I plotting to dress up my little brother as a Backstreet Boy or Kid. Thank goodness YouTube didn't exist when I was growing up, because the silliness of my younger self might have prevented me from moving forward in my professional career in my 30s. My dad was a guidance counselor, so I didn't have much rope as a firstborn going through my teenage years. Now, with a pre-tween myself, I hear echoes of, "Whatever you dish out, you'll get back tenfold." Oh, how true this is. Apparently, I was a little bit sassy.

I like to think I'm still sassy today. Most of all, I spent my life believing that if I did "everything right," it would be my path to safety and security. If I got a good job, secured a pension, married a nice guy, invested in my Registered Retirement Savings Plans (RRSPs—Canada's equivalent of 401(k)s for my American friends), saved for a rainy day, and avoided debt at all costs, I would be set. Life would be good. This was well-intentioned advice from my parents, family, friends, and society—those who believed money was either scarce or simply meant to make you comfortable. Scarcity, or comfort, was the name of the game, and getting a good deal was a celebrated event.

Ultimately, there was an underlying belief that money was scarce and very hard to come by and, more importantly, that you could lose it at any moment. As a result, my life became all about calculating risk. To ensure I made the "right" decisions and took the "right" steps at the right moments, I played not to lose at every turn so that someday I, too, could achieve the dream of the white picket fence, which we all seem to chase. That coveted white picket fence where you get married, have children, drive a minivan, and have a professional career—somehow, this equals having it all.

I went to college and got a degree—straight A's, of course—then doubled down on security by getting my MBA. I finally got a credit card and made sure to pay it off every single month. I landed a good job in the government with a pension, which, of course, was celebrated by all. Last but not least, I married the "nice guy." Everything was on the up and up. I was checking off the checklist, one item at a time, doing all the things I thought would lead me down the red carpet to success and the white-picket-fence dream. By society's standards, I was making good progress, celebrated by my family and others. Until one day, I woke up and realized I was incredibly unhappy.

It turns out that finding a "nice" life partner wasn't enough. It wasn't enough to make it work in a truly long-lasting union. I had given birth to my first child, and my partner and I were on different planets in terms of desires, expectations, and, ultimately, life. Next thing you know, I found myself in the midst of a terrible divorce and a single mom. Make no mistake—these were my "Spiritual Smackdown" days.

I questioned everything. I didn't know who I was anymore, didn't know how to step forward, didn't know what "good" looked like, and, at all points, I was definitely not comfortable. I'll spare you the details of my divorce out of respect for the father of my child, but I will say that coming from a family whose parents had been together for eons, this was not something I had ever considered a real option. I felt deeply alone and ashamed. My parents, of course, supported me no matter what, but I still carried an overwhelming sense of shame, guilt, and failure. It was almost physically heavy at times and felt insurmountable. I had moments where I honestly didn't know if I could go on. It was challenging, and some days were very dark. It felt as though the universe was showing up and giving me all the things I was terrified of. A little universal booming voice saying, *"I am the universe. Let me give you all the things you fear so you know you can overcome them."* Argh—how do I fast-forward through this part? Inevitably, the only way through was straight ahead—through the difficult parts, holding myself together as I balanced on the tiniest beam of hope.

Within months of my divorce, I also lost my "supposed-to-be-forever golden ticket" government job with a pension. I was devastated. It wasn't enough that I lost my marriage—then the universe handed me a pink slip for my job. The universe really has a way of showing up with resistance when you need it—nothing like a little extra kick in the ribs when you're already down.

There were days when I woke up feeling sick to my stomach. Every two weeks, I'd open emails from my lawyer with invoices for $2,500 or more. That's a hefty bill for an unemployed single mom. At that time in my life, I genuinely felt that debt and divorce were the two things I feared most, and here I was, standing knee-deep in the middle of both.

Since I was taught that debt is bad, I really questioned who I was. I lost weight, shed millions of tears, and had panic attacks in the middle of the night. It was truly the dark night of my soul.

Despite that, clinging to my tiny ray of hope, I managed to purchase a small home for my son and me with the proceeds from our marital home. Many people at the time told me not to buy a house—rent instead since I didn't know where I was headed. Thankfully, I had enough sense to trust my intuition and ensure I had a stable, grounded place for my son and me to thrive post-divorce. I was now a single mom, and my only job was to make sure he and I were safe. The rest didn't matter.

I remember one night after we moved into our new house, the whole house was quiet as a mouse. My son was tucked safely into bed, and I sat in the living room with the window open. The crickets were chirping outside, and I sat with myself in grief. That's how I'll explain it. It felt like I was losing who I was. How in the heck did this happen? I thought if I did everything according to the playbook of the white picket fence, I was supposed to be secure, that it would all work out, and I would get my dream. Instead, I ended up with a mountain of debt, a divorce, no job, and single motherhood. By the way, shout out to single moms—you are fortified badasses!

In the weeks that followed, I looked into my young son's eyes. I vividly remember being in the backyard, spinning him around, and having a moment of clarity. I realized that all that truly mattered was what I already had—my health, my happiness, my son, and the grass under my feet. But I knew that I had to change the way I had been living. As I looked into his eyes, I knew my job was to change how we lived, to change the way we connected to money, and to have more choice to live the way we wanted to. I had to stop playing "not to lose" and start playing "to win." I realized I needed to find another way, and maybe—just maybe—I needed to reconsider the rules of this white-picket-fence game and whether it was even what I actually wanted.

After many tears, personal development, prayers, sleepless nights, therapists, spiritual ceremonies, and moments of alignment, I made a decision. Slowly, brick by brick, I rebuilt who I was. I came back to the heart of who I truly was and discovered what actually brought me joy versus what the world told me I needed to acquire and achieve. I remembered that life is full of infinite possibilities, but playing to win is very different from playing not to lose. I was ready to transcend that white picket fence. I decided that there was more to life than just getting on the hamster wheel of a nine-to-five job to obtain that white picket fence, that perfect house, and that beautiful minivan. I realized that what I truly wanted was the precious gift of living life to its fullest.

It was that moment of decision that changed my life.

It was the permission to explore who I really was—not from societal expectations, not from the expectations of how to do things, and not from a checklist of "if I do A, B, and C, I will get X, Y, and Z." But to really live from a place of how I felt. Did the decisions I made bring me joy? Did they make me feel good? Did they bring me happiness? These became the questions most pivotal to my soul and guided my steps slowly back to life.

So, where am I today? Today, I'm a joyful mother of three boys. Yes, I went on to have two more, and I'm happily remarried to my soulmate—thank goodness we finally found each other. And incredibly, I'm a first-generation multi-millionaire. That's right—multi, not just one. I don't do things I don't enjoy, and I constantly check in with myself to ensure that what I am doing aligns with my deepest knowing and heart's center. My focus is always on growing and leaning into the infinite potential of the universe. I spend intentional time reflecting on what brings me joy and anchor myself in gratitude every single day. I play to win and take brave steps rather than focusing on the "right" ones. I work to create passive income and build wealth that has given me the freedom of both time and money. This has brought incredible freedom of choice for my family and my children. I actually feel free. I've transcended that white picket fence because the white picket fence is no longer the goal.

I feel free to choose. I'm in charge of my destiny, and I know deep in my soul that I'm meant to help women heal their relationship with money so they, too, can embrace a paradigm shift and be empowered to live life on their own terms—a life that transcends the current white picket fence that society tells you you need.

I often reflect on how people say that money doesn't buy happiness. After much reflection, I agree, but money sure as hell buys power and freedom of choice. And women, more than ever, need choice. In a world still riddled with inequality and gender bias, women must have avenues to create education, empowerment, knowledge, and confidence. I believe that a world where conscious women hold more money will change the world for the better. I imagine a moment where every woman on the planet is the matriarch of her own money, where she makes money her *employee* and knows, deep in her soul, that money can work for her to build the life she envisions whilst holding her feminine energy of receiving simultaneously. As women, we're constantly told by society and others that we shouldn't make too much or too little. We shouldn't be too pretty, and we should be humble at all costs. We're certainly not supposed to talk about how much we make or how we make it.

As a sisterhood, I believe we need to change that. It's not possible to ignite a paradigm shift without talking about money, without normalizing conversations about wealth in the hands of women. We need to create open spaces to have these discussions—about debt, money, wealth creation—and how we, as a sisterhood, can change the way we look at money for generations to come. I truly believe that more money in the hands of great women will change the world for the better. If I can go from $50,000 in debt to a multi-millionaire in less than five years, so can you. I know you can because I did it too. You might be thinking, *It's not possible for me,* but I assure you, as someone who came from no money, a scarcity mindset, and single motherhood, you can do it too. Look at me as an example: You, too, can build financial freedom, happiness, and sustainable wealth and shift your life and the generations that come after you. It's not just about a physical passing of money, but a profound shift in mindset. You need to heal your relationship with money and make room for something new. It's time to get off the oppressed hamster wheel and look beyond that white picket fence into the infinite possibilities that exist for you too.

My discipline and career path for the past 20 years has been in marketing and branding. Despite this formal knowledge, I've always been really attracted to entrepreneurial endeavors. In 2017, I found myself with an opportunity to work with a small, growing insolvency firm. I was drawn to them because they were passionate defenders of financial fairness in a way I hadn't seen before. They expanded my perspective on the banking system, creditors, and money in a way that was different from my previous understanding. They believed in second chances for individuals in debt and understood intuitively that your financial situation does not define who you are. In other words, they didn't judge a book by its cover. And the founder was a spitfire of a human being—he wasn't afraid of anything, and I loved his passion to play to win. It was unique and refreshing to see someone who turned his dreams into reality, paying little attention to red tape to get things done.

As their newest vice president of marketing, my first task, as any good marketer knows, was to understand their client base. I needed to truly understand these clients who were in need of serious debt relief: how they ended up in that situation and what they sought from an insolvency firm. So, I decided to contact a local research firm to conduct customer focus groups. We invited a variety of individuals to the discussion: current clients, potential clients who might need help, and clients who had filed with competitors.

I vividly remember sitting behind that one-way glass pane, notebook in hand, ready to soak up everything these individuals were about to share. As I sat in that little room listening to everyone speak, I was gobsmacked to realize that we are all a little closer to both wealth and insolvency than we like to imagine. More often than not, I heard stories of divorce, identity theft, fraud, job loss, critical illness, and addiction. It became clear that, in most cases, it wasn't a lack of a rainy-day fund, but rather an unexpected event that led to financial hardship. It became clear to me that we're all a bit closer to both edges of the financial sword than we think. It wasn't just about good investing or financial awareness—it was about navigating external circumstances and, to some extent, luck.

It took me a while to process this. It's easy to think that what we have and do in this world is entirely a result of our choices. But the role of something greater—like God, Luck, universal intervention, whatever you believe in—was harder to wrap my head around. Yes, we are creators of our destiny, but there is also an element of universal intervention and guidance. With wealth, you can be lucky enough to be in the right place at the right time, meet the right person, have the right coffee, or say the right thing. And with debt, you can be in the wrong place at the wrong time and make the wrong decision at the wrong moment.

What surprised me most was that these clients weren't the deadbeats society often paints them to be. They were entrepreneurs, accountants, blue-collar workers, nurses, doctors, coaches, and teachers. They could be anyone. As a marketer, we're often told to identify an ideal client profile, but I couldn't walk away with a single one—except that they all found themselves in crushing, unexpected debt without the ability to pay it back.

Anyone can find themselves in debt, just like anyone can become wealthy. This realization was profound for me. Some of these clients even drove fancy cars, owned beautiful houses, or ran multiple businesses. This challenged my previous belief that if you looked rich, you were rich. Outwardly, some painted the picture of wealth, but on paper, they had nothing and needed help. This realization turned my world upside down in an instant. What these focus groups taught me went beyond identifying an ideal client—it completely changed my perspective.

Wealth is actually what we can't see. On the surface, many of these people had what others would deem "rich," but on paper, they were completely insolvent.

It was a stark lesson and reminder that you truly can't judge a book by its cover. So, the next time you're scrolling through Instagram, do yourself a favor and remind yourself that just because someone had a $100k month doesn't mean they didn't have $99,000 in expenses. Or that just because they drive a fancy car, it doesn't mean they can afford it, that it's paid off, or that it's not a liability. In essence, *looking* wealthy doesn't automatically mean you *are* wealthy. In fact, many exceptionally wealthy people don't fit this definition at all and instead opt for modest cars and attire.

This is a huge disconnect. As humans, we make decisions about whether people are wealthy based on what we see—or don't see. What we see on social media is not necessarily an accurate reflection of net worth or what money someone truly has. I'm not immune to the glitz and glamor plastered all over social media or even in society in general. We're constantly comparing where we are with others, but we don't get to see their true net worth or their level of happiness. We don't get to see their monthly cash flow or whether they feel aligned and joyful on a daily basis. We don't get to see the inner workings of their financial situation.

We don't get to see their debt. We don't understand why they have or don't have something. We don't get to understand the motivation behind their choices. There's a big difference between looking rich and truly being wealthy.

I don't fault anyone, though. We make the best decisions we can with the information we have. The problem is we don't have all the information, and our reasoning is not perfect for any number of reasons. Unless we start sharing our net worth statements and cash flow statements—which is unlikely—we'll probably never have all the information. And let's remember, those who are truly millionaires are likely not the ones posting on social media trying to *show* how rich and wealthy they are. Truly wealthy folks don't need that validation and are too busy creating world impact with their time to worry about showing off their new *purse.* They also know deeply that wealth is far more than fancy, shiny things—it's not something you can see, steal, or take away. It is truly a summation of all their assets minus their expenses, along with world impact and internal gratitude for building a life they love.

They're not looking for someone to validate that they're wealthy. They're not necessarily buying the fancy purse or the luxury car to show off—they're doing it because perhaps they want to, or it brings them joy. Maybe they're in the luxury car business, or maybe it simply brings them happiness to take a spin in a fancy car after a long day. Purchasing something expensive and beautiful for joy is entirely different from doing so for validation or recognition.

Food for thought: As you compare yourself on social media, remember it's never as simple as "one plus one equals wealth." It's not simply about driving a fancy car or having a big house, and therefore you're wealthy. That's just not the case. My time working with individuals deep in debt showed me that every single day. We rarely get the full story.

So, it's time for you to write your own. Stop comparing yourself to standards that likely aren't even what you desire. Instead, begin your own journey to wealth—one defined by you. One where you understand that wealth is not just about the financial side of your net worth statement or about *looking* rich to others but about blazing your own trail to joy and happiness every single day. Where money becomes the enabler of a life built around your deepest desires.

BEING A MILLIONAIRE

There are so many different uses of the word "millionaire" on the internet, so it's hard to know what being a millionaire actually means.

Is it because I make seven figures a year?

Is it that I have seven figures in assets?

Is it because my company has over seven figures in revenue?

This is really about level-setting. So, let's level-set, shall we?

In short, a true millionaire is someone with a net worth of at least $1 million. It's a simple math formula: assets you own minus the liabilities you have equals more than a million dollars. That's it—you're a millionaire. This doesn't necessarily mean you have a lovely house, a fancy car, jet planes, or even that you are happy (we'll get to that in a later chapter). It's just a simple net worth calculation. Basically, if you shut it all down today, there's a million dollars that falls out.

Okay, perhaps at the moment, a million-dollar net worth feels far off. But if you're reading this book, you're already on the way to becoming the first joyful millionaire in your family. Just picking this up and starting to plant the seed that it is a possibility for you, too, is huge! But you may have some doubts. You might be thinking, *Me? Could I do this? Really? I didn't grow up with money. I didn't experience it. I don't know how to necessarily make more.* You likely have some reasonably good financial habits, but deep down, you're probably wondering, *Can I do this too? No one in my family has had money before. How could I become a millionaire? I don't have wealthy parents, and I don't even know what it takes.* But I have really good news for you.

According to the National Study of Millionaires carried out by Ramsey Solutions, 79% of millionaires in the U.S. did not receive any inheritance from their parents or family members. So drop those doubts at the door and step into it—yes, this is 100% possible for you. This is not something that's just out there and unavailable. This can be available for you too. If you didn't come from money, there's an overwhelming probability that you can actually achieve millionaire status as well.

The study also revealed that one in five millionaires, or 21 percent, received only a little inheritance, and only 3% inherited a million dollars or more. Sure, some folks had a leg up, but the point is most millionaires didn't come from money. So while you might think becoming a first-generation millionaire is difficult or impossible for you, reading this book is the first step toward making that a reality for yourself. Yes, some millionaires out there had some money to start with, but most didn't. And that's good news for you if you're thinking it's not possible—because it is. Whether you had money or didn't, it doesn't matter. It doesn't matter your circumstances, what you grew up with, or what your money mindset is. You have this possibility, and the statistics show it. Just by the numbers, if you didn't come from money, becoming a millionaire is not only possible for you. Today, the biggest thing I want you to decide is that you, too, can become a joyful first-generation millionaire.

Is becoming a first-generation female millionaire something you desire, believe in, and are committed to? I need you to decide today—with a big "Hell, yes." Don't move on from this chapter until you've decided that it is possible and probable for you, too.

While we'll get into money more later in this book, what's really important at this moment is to commit to the decision that this is something you desire and that you're willing to do the work to understand that it's not just about how it looks, but about building generational net worth in a way that is joyful, aligned, and connected to your core desires.

If you stick with me in this book and do the work, the actions, and the exercises, this, too, is possible for you.

Almost 80% of millionaires started exactly where you are. You might be feeling some fear, but I'm giving you a pass on that as well. You don't need to have it all figured out. Just decide with deep belief that it is possible for you.

I have no fear for you because I did it too. I, too, was a woman who came from no money. My parents provided me with a solid upbringing —which you will learn more about in later chapters—but I didn't come from wealth or overflowing abundance by any stretch. I largely grew up with a scarcity mindset, or as I like to call it, a "comfort mindset." But there came a moment when I had to believe in possibility. It was when I looked into my son's eyes, terrified as a single mom. In that moment, I needed to acknowledge the possibility—I had to believe that I could provide him with a different future, a different life, a different possibility than I had. Not just for him, but for me, and for all the future generations behind us. Becoming the first millionaire in your family starts with choosing it. It is a choice.

PERSONAL REFLECTION QUESTIONS

Below you will find some reflection questions with space to write your answers. Be sure to find a quiet space and complete these questions and activations before you move on to the next chapter. This will ensure you get the most you possibly can out of this book, and not only take in the information but activate it in your life.

1. What does true wealth mean to me?

_____

_____

_____

_____

2. What feelings come up when someone tells me I can be the first millionaire in my family?

_____

_____

_____

_____

3. Do I believe I can become a first-generation joyful woman millionaire? Why or why not? What are the things that might be holding me back? What could boost my belief in this?

_____

_____

_____

_____

4. How have societal expectations of appearance and status influenced my perception of wealth?

_____

_____

_____

_____

5. In what ways have I observed the pressure to appear wealthy impacting my financial decisions?

_____

_____

_____

_____

6. What are some steps I can take to prioritize building my net worth over merely looking wealthy?

_____

_____

_____

_____

7. In what ways can focusing on net worth over appearance-based wealth contribute to my overall financial security and independence?

_____

_____

_____

_____

8. How can I balance societal expectations of looking wealthy with my personal values and financial priorities?

_____

_____

_____

_____

9. What is my current net worth? (If you haven't calculated your net worth before, you can access a free net worth calculator at quantum-femmewealth.com)

_____

_____

_____

_____

10. What decisions have I made that have contributed to and increased my net worth? What decisions have led to a decrease in net worth? What does this teach me?

_____

_____

_____

_____

ACTIVATIONS

1. Decide that it is *possible* for you to become a joyful first-generation woman millionaire. Remember: It starts with a choice.

2. Once you decide, write the following affirmation on a piece of paper and stick it in a place where you will see it multiple times a day: *"I am the first woman millionaire in my family. I am wealthy, happy, and abundant. Money flows to me like an unending river."*

3. Each time you see this affirmation, I want you to say it out loud. (Yes, out loud.)

4. Record this affirmation on your phone and play it to yourself each morning as you wake up (before you hit your scroll).

5. Calculate your current net worth (head on over to quantumfemmewealth.com to access my free net worth calculator). It's really important to understand where you are today so you can see what is increasing or decreasing your net worth.

6. Once you calculate your net worth, reflect on which things in your life are bringing money to you (assets) and which are taking money away (liabilities).

To make things easy,
access the Quantum Femme
wealth website

SCAN THE QR CODE:

SCAN ME

CHAPTER 2

Money is Not a Dirty Word

"You either master money, or, on some level, money masters you."
–Tony Robbins

My grandfather's name was Guy. He was an entrepreneur—maybe he passed those genes to me—and also the grandfather I never got to meet. He met my grandmother, Daisy, and was quickly taken by her. They ran off to be married in a quick fashion and years later found themselves with a family of 15 children. My dad was number 13 in the pecking order. My grandpa owned and operated a dry-cleaning business and, by all accounts, was a wealthy man who connected with the business professionals in town, ensuring their clothes were always crisp and fresh. My grandparents lived in a big, beautiful old house. It was red, had a wraparound porch, and was located in Eastern Canada. Back in their heyday, they hosted glamorous parties, had maids to attend to their every need, and could afford to send their older children to boarding school—a very big deal, especially for the women in the family.

Unfortunately, in the midst of raising their family, tragedy struck.

Their big, beautiful home burnt down to the ground. My grandfather, as savvy as he was, didn't have home insurance. You can imagine how devastating this was for my dad's family. Despite having a thriving business, 15 kids, and facing a major financial blow, they suddenly had to figure out how to manage money for the first time.

They went from having much abundance to scarcity in almost an instant. Children were pulled from private school, and times became very tough. Money was scarce. The kids had to work to bring money in, and my grandfather struggled deeply. He felt immense shame and guilt.

For the first time in his life, he connected money to his worthiness and well-being. Unfortunately, he turned to alcohol, as many do when facing difficulties to drown his pain. When my dad was 17, my grandfather died. In an instant, my father witnessed not only the loss of money but also the loss of his father and their family's wealth. You can imagine how, as a young child, this shaped his mindset about savings, risk, and comfort. For my father, money quickly became a dirty word. It had taken their business, their happiness, their wealth, and, sadly, his father. Consequently, my dad's mindset became about saving, comfort, and avoiding risk, and you can see why. He wanted to avoid the pain that money could bring, and he certainly didn't want to lose it.

As a parent myself, now with three children, I think everyone who has kids can relate to the desire to protect them, to teach them, and to ensure they're resilient. Having gone through what my father experienced, his mindset about money became that it could be lost and that it could bring pain. For him, the money game became about comfort, saving for a rainy day, and making decisions with as little risk as possible. He didn't want me to experience the pain he endured when his father lost their money.

It wasn't until my recent work in wealth and money that I really started to better understand and reflect on my own money mindset and programming or even acknowledge that it was there. In fact, much of the time we are on autopilot—running our lives based on subconscious programming we received without even realizing it.

As a society, we don't have a universally agreed-upon standard of what "good" looks like when it comes to money, financial freedom, or even happiness. We don't all get the same education about money, or even the same ideas or perspectives on it. We aren't taught how to manage a mortgage, understand interest rates, or invest. We're certainly not taught how to be entrepreneurs. We're taught how to be employees, but there's no formal financial "university." So, how do we learn about money? It quickly dawned on me that, at the end of the day, we learn our money habits from our parents, guardians, society, and the environment we grow up in. We either have parents who explicitly teach us about money—or not.

In either case, we learn something.

Sometimes, we just observe. Perhaps we saw our parents fighting over money, never talking about it, or sharing their financial troubles. It doesn't really matter what you saw; in every instance, you learned something, and it became a belief—a program you downloaded deep into your unconscious without even realizing it. You associated what you saw with the truth about money. Perhaps you learned that money was shameful, caused disagreements, or was a source of stress. Or perhaps you learned that buying things helped you feel better or fit in. No matter where you are, we all have generational money beliefs and programming.

If you want to become the first millionaire in your family—and we know you do, because you wouldn't be this far into the book if you didn't—you need to understand what your existing programming is. You need to get real about what your money beliefs, money mindset, and money blocks are. You'll need to spend intentional time considering which beliefs serve you and which ones are holding you back.

Money beliefs are ideas, thoughts, or opinions that impact your money behavior. A money belief can be either protective or liberating. Money beliefs are common to all of us—we all have them. Yet, one person's beliefs can be vastly different from another's. A money mindset is the overriding attitude you have about finances, built on your overall beliefs. It drives how you make key financial decisions every day, and it can have a big impact on your ability to achieve your goals. If you change your mindset about money, you tend to make better choices and can overcome challenges. Lastly, money blocks are usually fears, self-limiting beliefs, or negative emotions that stand in the way of your financial success. You may not even be aware they're there. And money blocks can sabotage you in very sneaky ways—either through action or lack of action—but either way limits you from your financial goals. They can lead you to make choices that aren't in the best interest of your business or your life without you even realizing it.

Examining your beliefs, your mindset, and your money blocks is an essential step to uncovering which ones you want to address, and which ones you want to rewire, to ensure that money flows more easily into your life.

Sometimes, it can be hard to identify these beliefs because they're locked away in our subconscious or simply part of how we operate. Over the years, I've not only seen hundreds of thousands of clients talk about their finances, but I've also had the opportunity to coach many amazing women in wealth. There are some common money beliefs I've heard repeatedly, and I want to share some of those with you. You might have heard some of these before, and that's okay—let's just explore them for now.

1. Money is the root of all evil.
2. Never talk about money.
3. More money, more problems.
4. Debt is bad.
5. I'm not good with money.
6. Rich people are assholes.
7. Money is a dirty word.
8. Save for a rainy day.
9. Money doesn't grow on trees.
10. A penny saved is a penny earned.
11. Money doesn't buy happiness.

These are just some of the most common ones. Looking at this list, do you resonate with any of them? Have you heard any of these growing up? If we examine this list together, which beliefs do you think might be holding someone back from becoming a first-generation millionaire? All of them? Some of them? Which beliefs might be blocking someone from the flow of money?

For example, if you want to become a millionaire but believe that rich people are assholes, we're going to have a problem. Either you become a "rich asshole" or a "poor nice person." That's a lose-lose situation.

I'm guessing you'd much rather be something in between—a grateful, first-generation woman millionaire. If that's the case, you'll need to address, release, and rewire any beliefs that may be holding you back. You need to deeply know that "money in your hands is good for the world" and that money is *not* a dirty word.

Now that's a belief I can get behind.

Addressing your money beliefs is so important because they shape how you show up, both consciously and unconsciously, with money. They influence how we act, feel, and behave. And frankly, you'd better make sure that what you believe is what you want to be true. Because if you believe it, it will likely drive your actions and, consequently, your life.

Sometimes, these beliefs sneak up on us and hold us back. I want to share an example about a client. We'll call her Sarah.

Sarah grew up in a household where money was largely a source of disagreements. It caused a lot of frustration and arguments between her parents. I think many of us can relate to this. Naturally, Sarah became a peacemaker and often felt like she had to mediate and reduce conflict.

What do you think Sarah learned from this? At a young age, she quickly learned to put her needs and desires aside to mediate family arguments. She learned that her needs were secondary to others and that money was *bad*—it caused arguments and wasn't good. It was stressful and used as a weapon in disagreements.

When Sarah came to me, she was struggling with her business and, more importantly, with putting her own needs first. Diving deep, trusting her intuition, and allowing herself to build the life of her desires seemed almost impossible. Can you see why?

We often live out our money stories. They become so ingrained in who we are that we don't even question them. Resistance and money blocks hide out as guilt or shame, and they hold us back as we try to build the life we desire. What I'm trying to point out is that we all have generational money stories, and I encourage you to think about yours. Think about it from a storytelling perspective. Consider your life—what would a movie about your money story look like? What about your parents' lives? Can you see why certain beliefs show up, especially when you understand their upbringing more deeply? What events shaped them?

Taking time to reflect on your own journey will give you insight into some of the programming you might have. It will also help you identify beliefs that you may want to drop, remove, or choose not to perpetuate in your life. And if you don't know the money story of those who raised you, ask! Through this exploration, you'll gain a new perspective on why you hold certain beliefs, and then you can decide if you want to keep them. Some beliefs may serve you, while others may be holding you back. You can examine the things you've heard and decide which ones to leave behind and which ones to carry with you as you build your first million.

There's been a lot of work done on money mindsets, but in my work, I've observed that people usually fall into one of four key categories:

1. **Wealth Mindset**. Those with this mindset habitually focus on adding world value and leveraging resources. They see opportunity and resources all around them and often own cash-flowing assets and businesses. They look at time, money, skills, and technology and are constantly driven to leverage them to create more value and offerings. Their focus is always on getting money to work for them, not the other way around. They aren't focused on saving but on

leveraging and value creation. They have laser-focused efforts with both time and money.

2. **Comfort (also known as Scarcity) Mindset**. This is someone who is focused on saving and comfort. These are the people who play not to lose. This was me before my universal intervention and Spiritual Smackdown. When they get money, they save a portion and live on the rest. They usually have large savings and could survive for a reasonably long time on what they've saved. The large savings makes them feel safe, and they are often very reluctant to reduce this "savings stockpile," as it helps them regulate. You'll often hear them talk about their rainy-day fund and paying off their house as the holy grail of achievement. They're uncomfortable with leverage and prefer to keep everything safe in the comfort of a savings account. They'll often say things like, "Don't invest anything you can't afford to lose," and typically invest in low-risk stocks and funds with low returns.

3. **"Day-to-Day" Mindset**. This mindset is characterized by living paycheck to paycheck. These are individuals who prioritize covering their expenses and spending the rest. People with this mindset focus on living for the moment. When money comes in, they allocate it and usually stop spending when it's gone. They love to indulge, but are careful not to go into too much debt for these indulgences. They make sure to pay all their fixed expenses first and avoid spending more than they have. They live paycheck to paycheck, without savings for a rainy day, but they likely won't go into debt to overindulge. With this mindset, they often have reasonably good budgeting habits and sometimes use an envelope system.

4. **"Live for Today Debt" Mindset.** These individuals habitually run on a debt mindset, meaning they often borrow and then spend. They tend to accumulate depreciating assets to *look* wealthy and are not focused on

net worth at all. They've already spent their time or money, and this pattern shows up in their bank statements: Money comes in and immediately goes out. They're often in the negative on a regular basis. You will often hear them say things like, "There's just never enough money." While there is a clear sense of scarcity around money, there's also a deep desire to live fully.

While there are many nuances to money mindsets, can you identify with any parts of these four? Do you fit squarely into one, or are there elements of each that resonate with you? Which one would you prefer to be based on where you are?

Your beliefs and mindset about money can either propel you forward or hold you back from becoming a first-generation millionaire. Once you understand these beliefs and your programming, you can assess which ones are serving you and which ones are not. Now you get to decide: Which beliefs do you want to keep? Which ones do you want to drop? Are there new beliefs and mindsets you would like to explore?

Moving toward awareness in your money mindset and beliefs can be emotionally charged. So be kind to yourself as you explore new options. For most of us, emotions, guilt, trauma, and shame are locked up deep around money. Yet, money is really nothing more than a socially created construct representing an exchange of energy. It's what we make it mean that makes it so hard for us to unravel our beliefs and mindset, making space for something new. You need to detach from the idea that money defines your reality and create space for the possibility that there's something out there you haven't yet tried. It's important to bring awareness to all of your money thoughts. Just reflecting on and documenting them can be the first step in identifying what may be holding you back.

The summation of our beliefs and mindset can leave us with money blocks as we seek to become first-generation millionaires. As women, we often underestimate our financial worth. We tend to undervalue our skills, expertise, and contributions in the workplace. We may negotiate for lower salaries or not negotiate at all, and we settle for less-than-optimal financial opportunities. This is how money beliefs can become blockers from reaching our wealthiest potential. These beliefs and blockers can often stem from societal conditioning or a lack of confidence. Sometimes, we also see financial dependence or a lack of independence. Historically, women have been socialized to rely on others for financial support, whether from a spouse, partner, or family member. This dependency can result in feelings of insecurity, especially in situations like the death or divorce of a partner, where a woman may find herself unprepared to manage her finances independently.

In my work as a women's wealth coach, many women have expressed feeling intimidated by financial planning and investing. This confidence gap is largely due to ingrained beliefs. As a result, women can miss out on opportunities to grow their wealth and secure their financial future. Many women also fear being perceived as "greedy" or a "b#$%" if they become wealthy. Media and society often portray Wealthy Women as unkind and lacking in humility or altruism.

While there are many challenges women face, I'm here to share one important thing: While it may take centuries for society to shift, the movement toward healthy money beliefs starts with one woman at a time. And you—yes, *you*—have the power to reflect, identify, and rewire your core money beliefs.

What I'm really trying to say is that there will always be reasons why you have limiting money beliefs. But you—and only you—are responsible for recognizing and rewiring them to shift your life toward becoming a joyful, first-generation woman millionaire. Addressing your money mindset is key to shifting a conscious pattern for all women.

A Bank of America study recently found that 94% of women believe they'll be personally responsible for their finances at some point in their lives. Whether that's due to being on their own or outliving a partner, the reality is that women typically live longer and will likely need to be financially independent. The issue, or disconnect, is that in the same study, only 48% of women noted they felt confident about their finances. So, while almost all women believe they will need to manage their own finances, less than half feel confident about doing so. Even more striking is that only 28% feel empowered to act.

The key takeaway: Yes, we lack a financial education framework in society, but we can't wait for someone to hand it to us. We must take the time to know our own stories, understand our beliefs, and lean in to learn more. We have to empower ourselves to act. If we want something different, we must do something different. We can point out that there's no financial fabric in place, or we can lean in to learn.

Another statistic I want to share specifically relates to investing, which often comes up with my wealthy clients. We know we should be learning about investing, but we don't get that education in school. The same Bank of America study noted that women are confident in managing everyday financial tasks, such as paying bills—92% said they're very confident. And 87% said they're very confident about managing a budget. Check, check—we've got those under control. However, only half (53%) are confident in managing investments, and only 44% are confident in creating a diversified portfolio. I see many women who come for wealth coaching looking for advice on how to invest, and the typical go-to is a financial advisor. Now, there's nothing wrong with that. But what I want you to acknowledge is that even if you're hiring a financial advisor, you need to understand enough about your investments to ask the right questions, keep them on their toes, and make sure you're getting everything you need from them—not to mention being aware of their fees and any hidden costs.

As women who are going to become first-generation millionaires, we must take on the responsibility to learn. No longer can we just point to the fact that we don't have that financial fabric or that we have unequal footing. This is true, but shifting this requires radical responsibility, and that is something we can do. With the advent of the internet, we now have access to information and data at our fingertips. We must give ourselves permission to ask questions, be honest about what we're learning, and seek out someone who has done it before us. There's a misconception in society that once we go through school and education, we stop learning after we graduate. This is not the path of a financially savvy first-generation woman millionaire. The joyful first-generation woman millionaire is always learning. She's always educating herself and never ashamed to ask questions.

She's always leaning into new knowledge, taking charge of her financial future, acknowledging when she doesn't know the answer, and finding it. She's asking the experts and getting into the right groups and circles.

While women and men have nearly equal influence on day-to-day financial decisions in their households, such as paying bills and determining the budget, less than half of those women feel they have influence when it comes to investment decisions. Only 46% of women feel like they have a voice, compared to 64% of men. The top obstacles holding women back from investing are lack of knowledge (32%), not having savings to invest (38%), and believing it's too risky (22%). While beliefs may be hard to change, accessing knowledge is something we can absolutely do.

Some other key findings in the study are noteworthy: Younger women are starting to pave the way for more open financial conversations. This makes me exponentially happy. Things are shifting. There is a paradigm shift happening, and it requires women to be at the helm—to lean in, to have the confidence to ask, and to invest in education and learning. To partner with coaches and leaders who've done it before them. This is our moment.

I want to acknowledge that we all have different upbringings, and some paths are more difficult than others. Some have more privilege than others, no question. But what I want to emphasize is that no matter where you are, there is a path forward. There's a step you can take. There's a question you can ask. There's a room you can get into. Money is power, money is choice, and women need that more than ever. Money is *not* a dirty word, so we better start talking about it.

PERSONAL REFLECTION QUESTIONS

Be sure to find a quiet space and complete these questions and activations before you move on to the next chapter. This will ensure you get the most you can out of this book and not just take in the information but activate it in your life.

1. What are three things you regularly heard growing up about money?

_____

_____

_____

_____

2. How have these things shaped your beliefs about money? What did they teach you?

_____

_____

_____

_____

3. Which of these beliefs are serving you to become a joyful first-generation woman millionaire?

_____

_____

_____

_____

4. Which of these beliefs are holding you back?

_____

_____

_____

_____

5. Which Money Mindset did you most resonate with? Is this the money mindset you would like to keep? Which one is your desired money mindset?

_____

_____

_____

_____

6. What area of your money management do you need to learn more about to feel confident in managing your money? How can you educate yourself more in these areas?

_____

_____

_____

_____

ACTIVATIONS

1. Write your Generational Money Story. What happened to your parents or guardians in their upbringing? How did this shape how they raised you?
2. Complete the "Clear Your Money Blocks in Three Easy Steps" exercise.
3. Write three new beliefs that will assist you in becoming a joyful first-generation woman millionaire.
4. Take the beliefs you want to rewire and write custom affirmations in the present tense ("I am...," "I have...") as if you already have all you desire. Write them on sticky notes or record them on your phone to listen to daily.
5. Buy the book or course, hire the coach, join the Quantum Femme Wealth Facebook group, and ask the question! ACTION is the key step here! You don't need to get caught up and feeling like you need to have the whole plan - just take action on your next most important step.

To sign up for our
free newsletter and
grab your FREE exercise

SCAN THE QR CODE:

SCAN ME

CHAPTER 3

You Better Want to Believe What You Believe

"Everything is energy, and that is all there is to it. Match the frequency of the reality you want, and you cannot help but get that reality. It can be no other way. This is not philosophy. This is physics."
–Albert Einstein

In 1992, *Aladdin* came out. I remember it vividly. Up until that point in my life, the name Jasmine was rather unique. Growing up in a small, relatively homogeneous city on the east coast of Canada, being different was exactly what I was trying to avoid. Consequently, I often thought about finding someone with the same name as me. Like most kids, I desperately wanted to fit in. I envied other girls who had more common names. I know it sounds silly now in hindsight—today, I love my name and all its meaning—but bear with me as I take you back to 10-year-old Jasmine.

It was almost impossible to find anyone with the same name, especially someone in my age bracket. So when *Aladdin* came out, my mom promptly decided to get us tickets. I vividly remember everything about that day. We picked out a beautiful dress, and I styled my hair in what I used to call the "pretty way" (half down, half up).

We walked into the movie theater, and I watched in complete fascination as the beautiful story of *Aladdin* unfolded before me. Not only did I see a character with the same name as me, but she was a princess —someone who looked like me, with dark hair, dark eyes, and olive skin. I felt like a celebrity just by sharing the same name as this dazzling Disney princess. The magic transported me entirely, and I felt euphoria in that movie theater that day. Not only did I feel like I fit in, but it was almost like I could step into a brand-new identity, one that was beautiful and royal. That feeling stayed with me for a long time. I was Jasmine—a Disney princess. This was the moment I decided I *needed* to go to Disney World.

I wanted to experience that magic again, to fit into this place where I didn't feel like I fit in anywhere else. I wanted to be closer to the magic I saw on screen—the magic that celebrated my name and made me feel like a princess. Keep in mind, though, that my family didn't have a lot of money. We were comfortable, not poor by any means, but with three children to care for, my parents had to teach us to be frugal and thoughtful about our decisions.

Going to Disney World wasn't exactly on the list of possibilities at that moment. I vividly remember telling my parents that I wanted to go, and my dad, in his usual frugal fashion, said it was a great aspiration but that we'd have to save money, work hard, and make sacrifices to go on such a big trip. However, he seemed open to the idea, and I was pleased. I began flipping through magazines, cutting out pictures of princesses, and putting them on little vision boards (as we'd call them today). I watched all the Disney VHS movies, and it was so much fun to imagine myself in a "whole new world" (pun intended).

I allowed myself to be transported into the magic of every movie I watched. I remember watching the screen and marveling at how creative the people behind them were. Somebody had to imagine the storylines, create the vision, and draw the beautiful characters, turning them into the movies I loved so much. I was in awe. We started a family jar to save money, and I'd put every extra coin and penny I had into it. I'd fall asleep at night imagining myself on a Disney ride, actually feeling the sensation in my belly as if I were going down a roller coaster, even though I hadn't been on one yet.

Disney World would visit my dreams, and I'd imagine smiling and meeting Princess Jasmine. I began telling my friends that we were going to Disney World, even before my parents confirmed it. I talked about the itinerary and told everyone what we were going to do.

Deep down, I knew that the delicious experience of meeting Princess Jasmine in real life was going to be mine. I had mastered the feeling of already being there, even though I had never set foot in Florida. Then, just after I turned 13—yes, three years later—my dad finally announced that we were going to Disney World. As a teacher, he planned to take us in August. We piled into our Lumina van and took an East Coast road trip down to the States. I was elated. It was as magical as I had imagined.

I vividly recall the memories of my family indulging in the magic of Disney World. I remember enjoying our packed lunch on the grass and listening to "It's a Small World" on repeat—my younger sister's ride of choice. It was everything I had dreamed of and more.

I can still close my eyes today and be transported back to that feeling. What I didn't realize at the time was that this experience was my first introduction to manifestation—something I've become exceptionally good at throughout my life. It was as if by putting my whole focus, beliefs, emotions, and trust into it, and acting as though I already had it, I could make it mine, regardless of what it was.

Chances are you've probably read the book *The Secret* at some point. It was a highly successful book that came out in 2006 and shed light on the idea that your thoughts create your reality, and that you can design your life, heal your life, and essentially manifest everything you want just by thinking you can. There's just one small issue: What if you don't really believe it? At least not completely, deep down in every part of your being. I think we can all relate to this feeling—when you put something on a vision board, make a to-do list, want something desperately, and yet, somehow, it just doesn't come true.

Because deep down, you don't believe you can make it happen, or you don't take the action required because you know it will be hard. Sure, you can put things on a vision board, cut out clippings, and repeat affirmations as part of your ultimate *someday* goal. But deep inside, with all the programming and beliefs you've picked up along the way, if you don't truly believe it can be yours—through your emotions, actions, and your entire vibrational frequency—then it's more of a hope and wish list than an inevitable part of your life.

Most of us are running around with old generational programming, and we don't even realize it. It's just hanging around like an old piece of furniture that we hardly notice anymore. We think we have new, innovative ideas, goals, and focus, but we're really just playing the same old playlist on repeat. Most of the time, we aren't even aware of what's holding us back. It's that sneaky. Most of our beliefs run in the background, and we never even notice or question whether they should be there. We just operate on that old track.

If you haven't heard of Human Design, it is one of those personality assessments that helps you navigate your natural gifts to maximize life a little more effortlessly. For those familiar with Human Design, I'm a 5-1 Responding Generator. This means I not only love leading people, but I truly enjoy investigating topics deeply. I love those moments when art and creativity intersect with something bigger, like science. Naturally, I was drawn to quantum physics and the science of manifestation. It fascinated me that everyone loved the idea of manifestation, but few truly understood the science and mechanics of what it was about. As you work toward becoming the wealthiest, most joyous version of yourself, there are fundamental scientific principles I want you to understand. If you grasp these, you'll have the keys to open the gateway to creating anything you desire. And I say "gateway" because knowledge is just the first step. It needs to be followed up with plenty of inspired action. So, let's dive in.

Early physics was split into two camps: matter and thought. The majority of scientific study focused on matter, not energy or thought. I remember learning about atoms in school. I'm sure you had a similar experience. As an investigator at heart, I studied atoms with much focus. My science teacher taught us that all things were made up of tiny atoms, and I internalized this idea as little pieces of matter. I could get behind that. I could wrap my head around the concept that everything in the world was made up of these teeny-tiny pieces of matter operating at different speeds. It's why I can touch my desk but cannot touch the light. We were taught about Newton's theory of the atom, this classic version where everything was predetermined and made up of small, predictable pieces of matter. This is despite the fact that Einstein's theory of $E=mc^2$ has been around for years.

For those who aren't familiar with $E=mc^2$, in its simplest interpretation, it means energy equals mass times the speed of light. At its core, the equation suggests that energy and mass (or matter) are interchangeable—they are different forms of the same thing.

Oddly enough, this wasn't part of my seventh-grade lesson. Instead, we went on to make a toothpick-and-Styrofoam-ball version of the atom for a science fair based on the idea of tiny, predictable particles. Of course, we got a little gold medal for it. But Einstein's discovery, despite not being included in my project, set off a new train of thought that connected energy and matter, giving birth to quantum physics. Today, we understand that the atom is not simply a collection of little pieces of matter, but is rather made up mostly of empty space.

That empty space is entirely energy. Everything in your physical reality is made not of solid matter but of fields of energy and frequency patterns of information. All matter is actually more energy than the predictable particles I learned about in my seventh-grade class. So, goodbye to the slow-moving desk particles!

But here's where it gets a little crazy. It's not enough for me to explain that everything is energy—you may already be aware of that. However, upon further study of the atom, quantum physicists realized that behavior at a subatomic level didn't align with the other theories of physics. In other words, the way atoms behaved wasn't as predictable as everything else in physics. The electron within the atom didn't move in consistent, predictable patterns. It gained and lost energy, appeared and reappeared, and didn't always follow the expected path.

I used to imagine an electron taking steps up to the top floor, but that's not exactly how it works.

In fact, these electrons showed up all over the place without regard to time and space at all. They disappeared and reappeared at their leisure. Quantum physicists were perplexed. Why did this happen? Until they discovered what we today call the **Observer Effect**. In its simplest form, this discovery showed that the very act of observing something affected the behavior and energy of matter, making it more predictable. What we now know through science is that the moment an observer observes the electron, there is a specific point where the probabilities of this electron move into physicality—where they become matter. This massive discovery proved that the mind and matter are indeed connected and that interacting with energy through observation allows it to move into physical form. This is also why quantum leaps are possible; time and space are not acknowledged at the atomic level, and it doesn't matter.

Deepening this idea further, **quantum entanglement** is another fascinating phenomenon from quantum physics where two particles become interconnected in such a way that the state of one particle is instantly linked to the state of the other, no matter how far apart they are. It's as if they share information instantly, defying the usual constraints of space and time. Let me give you an example:

1. Imagine you have two magic dice.
2. If these dice are "entangled," whenever you roll one, the outcome of the other is instantly determined, no matter where it is—whether in the next room or on another planet.
3. This happens because their properties are connected in a way that transcends the physical distance between them.

Quantum leaps, in science, refer to the sudden jump of an electron from one energy level to another within an atom. These leaps occur without the electron "traveling" through the space in between—it simply transitions instantly. From a **scientific perspective**, quantum leaps demonstrate that change doesn't always have to be gradual; it can happen suddenly and dramatically. AND, that small shifts in energy or intention can create significant, non-linear outcomes.

When we relate this to personal growth, success, or transformation, **quantum entanglement** suggests that we are interconnected with the universe and can influence outcomes in profound ways. **Quantum leaps** show us that radical transformations are not only possible but natural, provided the right energy, focus, or intention is applied.

Just as entangled particles influence each other and electrons make sudden leaps, we too can create significant shifts in our lives by aligning our energy, actions, and intentions with higher possibilities. This scientific metaphor reinforces the idea that extraordinary break-throughs are accessible, often without following a linear path.

Now, let me bring you back to the matter at hand (if you'll excuse the pun).

Simply put, what you believe, feel, focus on, observe, say, and how you show up—either consciously or unconsciously—affects the creation of your material reality. What you say to yourself, what you believe or disbelieve, whether aloud or just in your mind, it all matters. It's not just about saying affirmations, though that's a start. What truly matters is what you actually believe with all your heart, emotions, thoughts, and actions. All alignment within your being is important. You must imagine your desired reality, feel it, believe it with your whole being, and lean into it, taking inspired action toward it as if it's already yours. There has to be complete alignment with what you desire—your mind, body, soul, beliefs, emotions, and actions must be in sync. When you have doubt, negativity, or beliefs that are contrary to what you want, you now understand why this will limit you. This will allow you to activate both scientific principles, pulling into your reality what you desire faster than you ever imagined possible.

I once had a remarkable client. We'll call her "Erin." Erin was an executive at a high-profile company. By other people's standards, she had "made it." She was a woman at a high-level executive table, kicking ass and taking names. But there was one problem: She was deeply unhappy with her job. It felt like a soul-sucking limiter, and more than anything, she wanted to start an online business to help other women with their relationships. This was her deepest desire. We met regularly to discuss this dream, and I could see it was hers to have if she chose it.

She could leave her job in an instant and build the life of her dreams. But time and again, she stopped herself. She doubted herself. She questioned whether it was the right move. She hesitated about leaving the security of her job for something that seemed so uncertain.

She didn't want to trigger others. She feared people wouldn't approve. She needed proof that it would work—that it was the right choice. And she couldn't understand why people in her current side business weren't buying from her. Most of all, she needed to be sure that launching her business was the "right move." She wanted to launch her business but didn't want to disappoint anyone. She wanted to grow her business but stay at a comfortable income level.

In the end, she wanted something she believed she couldn't have, so she started limiting herself accordingly. She wanted to stay comfortable while also taking a risk for growth. Can you see why Erin never fully launched her online coaching business?

Can you see why she chose to stay in the job she hated so much? She wanted something, but she didn't believe it could be hers. She doubted herself, kept stopping herself, and suggested she didn't want to disappoint others when, in reality, she didn't want to disappoint herself.

Here's what I need you to know: The energetic science behind manifestation, the information I've shared with you, is more powerful than you can imagine. If you want to step into your highest, most wealthy, and joyful version of yourself, you must believe at your core that it is available to you. Not only available but *inevitably* yours. It is a conscious decision to shift. You have to intentionally examine your thoughts, beliefs, programming, and understanding of reality. You have to drop self-doubt and go all in—with a belief so strong that it overrides everything else, and your actions align accordingly.

By the way, this is an ongoing process. Every time you level up and desire something new, you will need to go through this process again. The Wealthy Woman's mindset is one of growth, happiness, and gratitude. It's about aligning your frequency, your being, and your actions with what can be yours, and holding steady in discomfort. It means that despite your circumstances, upbringing, programming, beliefs, or current situation, anything is possible for you. It's about giving yourself the space to believe that you, too, can become the first millionaire in your family. You must intentionally build thoughts and ideas that support the physical reality you desire. The universe is abundant with possibility, and how you think and believe—both consciously and unconsciously—can work for or against you. The beautiful thing is— you get to decide.

With this powerful information, you might be wondering how you can move forward. Neuroscientists tell us that 95% of our thoughts are controlled by subconscious pre-programming. If we weren't just playing that old track on repeat without questioning it, we'd be shifting our lives at will. You wouldn't fear money, you wouldn't feel lack, and you'd have complete faith in your potential. You'd be so ecstatically grateful all the time that you'd intrinsically know the universe supports you at every moment, and that every decision is working for your highest good.

In the end, what I need you to understand is that you must *want* to believe what you believe because that's the key to where you're headed. The science I've shared with you will help you bring forth whatever you believe, both consciously and subconsciously. What you truly believe, feel, and vibrate at will manifest as the physical reality in your world. So make sure your beliefs are ones you truly want to be true.

I sometimes refer to my internal track as either the gremlin or the cheerleader. You need to intentionally take a moment to think about the way you talk to yourself. Is it a gremlin? A voice that holds you back, maybe keeps you comfortable, casts doubt on your big ideas, and perhaps works to keep you small or avoid taking risks? Or is it your cheerleader—the one who stokes good ideas, reminds you that you've got this, and that the universe will show up no matter what? I encourage you to think about that. Do you have a gremlin or a cheerleader as part of your internal track?

If the answer is a gremlin, it's time to fire that ass hat and post a job opening for a new cheerleader. Be really clear about the type of role you're looking for in a cheerleader. It's essential to build a Wealthy Woman identity, and for that, you need your internal cheerleader by your side. Having a positive internal track will make it infinitely easier as you face growth head-on.

You must believe that you can do what you want to do without a shadow of a doubt. And to be clear, we are all human, so we will have wobbles in this. But you must have faith that it will work out. The exact opposite of fear is faith. Take a moment now to consider: What is your internal track on a daily basis? What do you worry about? What do you say to yourself? What might you do if you had faith that your vision would work out? I highly recommend you take time to listen to your internal track—both the cheerleader and the gremlin—to make sure things are moving in the direction of your ultimate desires.

Every time you level up, you might encounter something new. Every time you push into growth, new doubts might arise. You want to intentionally look at these. What are you telling yourself? What ideas are you holding on to? You can keep a journal, write down these thoughts, and identify which ones serve your cheerleader and which ones need to be fired along with the gremlin.

Getting your internal track and beliefs to align with your ultimate vision for your life is key. This shift will help align not only your beliefs but also your frequency, which means your desires become inevitable. Here are some ideas to help you activate these newly aligned beliefs and raise your frequency:

1. **Bring Your Vision into Physical Reality.** One of the easiest steps you can take is to get crystal clear on exactly what you desire. This is why vision boards or physical creations of desires are so popular. Everything is possible for you. Forget the *how* and just trust that it's already yours. Don't limit yourself by thinking it's not achievable. As humans, we tend to set smaller goals for fear that we won't achieve the bigger ones. But this time, check fear at the door and ask yourself,

What would I do if I believed? What move would you make if you had faith that it would happen? Take some sacred space to imagine what that vision would be for you. Write out a check for the money you desire, write a gratitude letter to yourself in the present tense thanking the universe for receiving all your desires, or create a vision board.

2. **Hire a Mentor or Coach.** One of the fastest ways to align new beliefs is to hire someone who has already done what you desire to do. They can expedite your timeline to achieve your goals and help identify areas where you may be limited and need focus. This will ensure you have someone who's always in your corner and can uplift you to new frequencies. They will have no fear for you because they've done it too and know it's possible.

3. **Join a Group/Follow Inspiration.** If you need to train your internal track to be more positive, consider joining a group that has already achieved what you desire to do. Surrounding yourself with people who can show you that it's a reality every day is a great way to show your body and brain that it's possible for you too! Whether it's a happier marriage, more money, real estate investing, becoming a first-generation millionaire, or something else—joining people who have achieved or desire the same thing can be very beneficial. Another easy way to do this is by following on social media those who have done what you desire. The beauty of the internet is how we can connect with like-minded individuals, regardless of location, and we can also curate our world on social media to consume *only* what helps bring our desires to reality. If you can't find a local group, see if you can find one online and be intentional about the individuals you follow.

4. **Imagine a New Identity.** As you uncover these beliefs and get clear on your desires, you may start to realize that a new identity is emerging for you. Consider the new identity you wish to create. Imagine for a second: who is the ultimate

person you want to become? It's important to identify exactly who that is so you can emulate that person even when you're not quite there yet. Having an internal guidepost or example of who you want to become can be very helpful when navigating decisions. For example, when I think about making decisions, I think about my future self or someone I admire. Ask yourself, *What would Steve Jobs do here?* or *What would Oprah do?* Or, if you have a clear enough picture of who you want to be, ask your future self, *What would future me do?* Starting to embody who you want your future self to become can be a very helpful exercise today. This also helps you become who you desire to be now— something the quantum loves.

5. **Try It On.** Once you know who you desire to become, one shortcut is to simply *try on* this new identity in spaces where no one knows you. Let me give you an example. I am a real estate investor, but there was a time when I only had two properties. The truth is, I was a real estate investor, even with just two properties under my belt. Of course, now I have many more, but back then, I would go to breakfast by myself, and when the waitress asked me what I did, I would confidently say, "I'm a real estate investor," long before I had the portfolio I have today. You can just try it on—bring that new identity into reality.

6. **Find Evidence.** The beautiful thing about our mind is that we have a confirmation bias. Even though we're only consciously aware of about 5% of our thoughts, with 95% running in the background, this bias helps us confirm things we already believe. So, if you want to shift toward becoming a Wealthy Woman, you need to start looking for evidence. Use your brain's hardwired confirmation bias to your advantage. Start looking for proof that you are what you want to become. You are a Wealthy Woman. Money *does* come to you. Whatever new belief you want to adopt, you can start to find evidence that it's true for you.

7. **Give Yourself Permission to Try Something New.**
Sometimes, we get so locked into what we like that we forget to open the door to see if there's something new we might like even more. Intentionally saying yes to something you wouldn't normally do can help you activate your discernment. Try it on and see if you like it. Keep what you like and discard what you don't. It's not a commitment; you're just trying it on. So, if you find yourself wanting to try something new, whether it's a new vision board or shifting from a lack mindset to a wealthy mindset, give yourself permission to tell yourself, *This week, I am the Wealthy Woman, and I'm going to operate as such.* Order exactly what you want for breakfast. Order exactly what you want when you go out to dinner. Ask for the dressing on the side, to hold the salt and to grill it just the way you like. These little things allow us to try on a new way of being. Take a new route home, or even say yes to something you'd usually turn down. And if someone gives you a compliment, simply say thank you instead of trying to be humble and not receive it.

8. **Determine Your Mission and Value-Driven Focus.**
Coaching women about money has been the most rewarding mission of my life. It has allowed me to drive incredible value, peace, joy, and gratitude for thousands of women. The wealth I feel from that far exceeds the energetic exchange of physical money in my life. Well-known author, motivational speaker, and high-performance coach Brendon Burchard once said, "If you create incredible value and information for others that can change their lives—and you always stay focused on that service—the financial success will follow." Deeply knowing the value you desire to create for the planet will help raise your wealth to new heights. Think about your *why*. Most people desire money, of course, but why? Money is just a tool—an energetic exchange for the value you bring to the planet. Think about the bigger, value-driven focus you

have for yourself. This will help you anchor into the bigger picture and operate from a level.

9. **Use Affirmations in Your Theta Brain State.** Our brains are more susceptible to ideas in some states of awareness than in others. Theta occurs just as you're waking up or falling asleep. This is a great time to introduce new ideas into your subconscious. One trick I use is to record present-day affirmations in my own voice on my phone and then listen to them first thing in the morning. So rather than rolling over and starting to scroll, you can listen to these Wealthy Woman affirmations and the new beliefs you want to download into your brain.

This understanding of the science behind manifestation, coupled with some practical ways to implement new beliefs, means that the power is now in your hands to make the conscious decision about what you believe or don't believe.

You actually now have the understanding that your beliefs are something that you can mold, shape, and form from energy to matter. It means that you can actually bring your dreams into beliefs, thoughts, and ultimately matter and reality to become the wealthiest version of yourself. The key is: what is it that you believe? And so in the next chapter, we're gonna explore what are some of the key belief codes that you can download to become the wealthiest version of yourself.

REFLECTION QUESTIONS

Grab the notebook that keeps your responses to these reflection questions all in one place, or jot down your answers below. Find a quiet space to contemplate answers, and let's activate!

1. What is it you deeply desire that has not manifested in your life yet?

_____

_____

_____

_____

2. Reflecting on this desire, what thought, emotion, action, or embodiment is out of line with your desires?

_____

_____

_____

_____

3. What piece of the scientific manifestation process do you think may be out of alignment with your deepest desires? What do you need to address? Consider your desire, emotion, embodiment, and daily actions. For example, perhaps you desire to start a business, but you are still working at a 9 to 5 job.

_____

_____

_____

_____

4. What are some steps and actions you could take today to bring forth your desires to more clearly and tangibly activate the science of manifestation and quantum energy?

_____

_____

_____

_____

5. What five attributes would you use to describe yourself? Now, how would you describe the wealthiest version of yourself—the joyful first-generation millionaire? Compare your lists. What is different? What is the same? What are the key areas you may need to bridge to become the wealthiest version you described relative to who you are today?

_____

_____

_____

_____

6. Is your internal track a gremlin, a cheerleader, or a mix of both? What does your internal track regularly tell you?

_____

_____

_____

_____

7. Does this internal track align with where you desire to go? Why or why not?

_____

_____

_____

_____

8. How can you change your internal track to align with your ultimate desires? Which activations would you like to try to align your new internal track?

_____

_____

_____

_____

ACTIVATIONS

1. Design the wealthiest version of you who has all her desires today. Be as clear as possible: What is she wearing? What does she drive? What does she do with her time? Who does she surround herself with? How does she make decisions?
2. Create a vision board with the items you imagine physically. This can be a digital board or physical clipping of the life you are dreaming of.
3. Spend the next week looking for evidence that money flows into your life. Record all the ways money and abundance flows in for you. It can be as small as finding a dime and as big as getting unexpected money in the mail. When abundance flows in, be sure to offer deep gratitude and praise to the universe.

CHAPTER 4

The Wealthy Woman Belief Codes

"The only way not to think about money is to have a great deal of it."
–Edith Wharton

I vividly remember the first day in my new little house that I had bought for my son and me following my divorce. I woke up on the floor, surrounded by a mess of blankets, boxes yet to be unpacked, and sunlight streaming through the window. I felt rested, without stress or the back pain I had been experiencing during the separation, and filled with utter gratitude for everything around me. It was almost overwhelming joy in my body. I was grateful for the air, the silence in my home, the warmth of the sun on my skin, and my son sleeping soundly in the next room. I finally had my own safe space for my son and me, and the rebuilding could begin.

I remember people showing up to help me move, feeling a bit of pity for me. I could sense it in the way they looked at me, spoke to me, and offered to help. It was a wonderfully elated moment in my life, but I could tell that my friends somehow felt sorry for me. After all, being a single mom is no walk in the park. Statistics show that single moms are more likely to be in debt, more likely to be considered poor due to low-income households, and more likely to experience food insecurity. But here I was, ready to start all over. While I was grateful for the support, I felt joy, not pity, for myself.

I remember waking my son up that morning with a kiss and scooting him downstairs to watch his Sunday morning cartoons. I popped some toast in the toaster, and I felt this deep sense of calm—a belief, a knowing that this was the beginning of something totally new, beautiful, and profound. I didn't have tons of money or things. By all accounts, I didn't have much at all. But somehow, I felt completely full of gratitude, abundance, joy, and overflow.

It was beautiful, raw, authentic internal abundance at its highest power.

I didn't know what the future held, but deep down, I knew we would be more than okay. We were safe and happy, and I had the opportunity to build a new life for us. I was grateful, not fearful. I didn't need anyone's pity because this moment was filled with pure joy and potential. I knew in my heart that I would change the narrative for my son around joy, happiness, and money. His story wouldn't be one of a broken home, but rather one of a strong, capable mother who showed him that anything was possible. That was my deep-seated belief, and I had an overwhelming sense of confidence, even when it didn't make sense to feel that way.

From that moment on, I went on a journey of healing and exploring my new identity. I gave myself space to try new things, say yes to things I wouldn't normally have said yes to, eat at new restaurants, go to concerts, spend nights in, look at my budget differently, and breathe in each little moment with deep gratitude. I kept what worked and left behind what didn't. I found a profound connection to my faith and the divine again. I connected to the source of who I was in a way I had never done before. I did so much healing work and found true happiness on my own as a single mom with my son.

Of course, there were lonely nights when I hugged my teddy bear, but I instinctively knew I wouldn't want to bring someone into this lovely little world I had created with my son unless it brought true joy.

About eight months later, my cousin and her partner came to visit for the first time since my divorce. My cousin and I were like sisters growing up. The three of us ended up at a little pub one afternoon while my son was at his father's place, talking about life and the possibility of me having a partner again. It seemed to interest them more than it did me. Let's remember, I hadn't dated in ten years, and now it was a whole different ball game. I had a son, so dating wasn't just for fun anymore. Things were a bit more important, a bit more serious.

On that fateful day, they introduced me to online dating—something I would have never explored before. But since I was in my "season of yes" and trying new things, I let them convince me to sign up and create a profile. Before I knew it, I had a few dates to consider and some interesting conversations happening. I made a promise to myself: If someone showed interest and I thought it was worthwhile, I'd go for coffee or a cocktail—and I'd always drive myself. If I didn't feel a connection, I would thank them for their time, pay for my beverage, and go on my merry little way. All joy—that's what I was looking for, and I wouldn't let it be anything else.

Fast-forward a few months later, I met the man who would become my future husband. I walked into a little pub for a date, feeling a bit grumpy. Dating wasn't as fun as I expected it to be, and I remember thinking that if this didn't work, I would leave early and enjoy the little family life I had created on my own. My son was with his grandfather, so if there wasn't a connection, I was ready to leave in favor of some snuggles with my little man.

That same sense of inner knowing, gratitude, and levity washed over me when my future husband walked in. He was tanned and trim, with a smile that lit up the room. Apparently, I earned bonus points for being early, as it caught him by surprise. We spent the rest of the evening talking and ended up closing the place down—which is impressive, given we met at 3 p.m. and the pub closed at 10 p.m. You know those moments when you just connect with someone? Time seems to melt away, and it's just the two of you. Somehow, we instantly knew we'd spend a lot of time together. He was thoughtful, interesting, curious, adventurous, and, most importantly, he saw having a son as a benefit, not a drawback or "baggage," as some less evolved men had suggested.

He intrigued me, and more importantly, we connected on a deeper level. He was divorced as well, so he understood the responsibilities I had as a single mom and the importance of marriage and true commitment. From a financial perspective, we were both career-oriented with a desire to build a family oriented life. We both came from loving families who are still together today. We had so much in common. We both loved travel and adventure and just wanted to live life to the fullest. We shared an insatiable desire to drink from the cup of life. We both had a growth mindset and similar desires for family and children. I knew in my heart, even on that first night, that he was the person I would be with for a very long time.

Over the years, we've walked through life inseparably. We've navigated tough times, including family dynamics, unexpected bills, growth, risk, and real estate, but one thing has always remained true: We made each other feel free, and together, we learned a new, soul-aligned way to generate joy and wealth.

We both had to learn and unlearn many things along the way. Today, as multi-millionaires, it's important to acknowledge that it took work to rewire the neural pathways that had been ingrained for years before we met. We had to download new belief codes, learn what we needed to believe in, and leave the rest behind. We engaged in continuous learning, challenging our thinking, and actively placed ourselves in rooms we had never been in before. I'm grateful to have a partner who has walked this season of life with me—the season of transformation from a single mom, who the world thought was destined for debt forever, into something I could have only imagined in my wildest dreams and absolute overflow. Over the years, it has been my deepest honor to walk through life with a man who shows me what true love is every day.

My love story aside, one thing I will say is that if you are in a relationship, wealth generation is infinitely easier if the person you're traveling through life with also sees joyful wealth as a priority. It doesn't need to be perfect—you will both have different money beliefs, blocks, and growth challenges along the way—but if you agree that wealth is a priority, it will be not only helpful but necessary. If you're not on the same page, it's a worthy discussion to have, as it will take effort and energy to shift your reality together. And if you're single—congrats! You get to call all the shots.

Throughout my journey to building wealth, I've refined and downloaded what I call **Wealthy Woman Codes**. These are deeply ingrained beliefs that form the basis of my decisions and actions on a daily basis. I'm sharing these 14 Wealthy Woman Codes with you as cheat codes for your own journey. Many of them came to me through trial and error. These are deep, ingrained beliefs I've cultivated over time to rise as the wealthiest version of myself. They are core tenets of my internal cheerleader and consistently help me point myself in the direction of my desires.

In many ways, I'm sharing a shortcut with you. Instead of going the long way, enduring a Spiritual Smackdown, and fumbling to learn the way forward, I hope these can help you shortcut your path to your desires. If you adopt them and consider how to embody and embrace them in your life, they can provide you with a gateway to becoming the wealthiest version of yourself.

Some of these may challenge your current thinking or beliefs. If resistance shows up, just notice it. I encourage you to remain open—to new ideas you may not have heard before, to a new download that could shift who you are today and propel you to a new reality. In the end, you are in the driver's seat. Take what feels aligned and leave the rest behind. So, without further ado, let's get going.

DEBT IS NOT BAD—IT'S JUST LEVERAGE

Here's the first one: There is a ton of shame around having debt in society, but debt, at its very foundation, is nothing more than a decision to pay something off over time. One of the first things you need to get your head around to become the wealthiest version of yourself is that debt is not inherently bad. In fact, for those who are wealthy, debt is actually leverage. You may have heard growing up that debt was bad—this belief will block you entirely from seeing any opportunities to leverage debt for investment or generating more wealth.

As the wealthiest version of yourself, you have to understand that you can use other people's money (i.e., debt) to create something better or generate more money. Let me give you an example. For our real estate ventures, we need to take on debt. We use some of our own money to access money from the bank (leverage)—I put down 20%, and they finance 80% of the home. I now have the property in my name, which we then rent out to someone else who pays the loan (mortgage). Not only did we leverage our initial money with money from the bank to access the property, but we also leveraged tenant money to pay the loan. Further, the property appreciates in value. This is leverage.

Leverage in the context of money refers to using financial tools or strategies to amplify potential returns or outcomes. It involves borrowing resources or using existing assets to increase the potential return on investment or to achieve a specific financial goal. While debt, in general, gets a bad rap, it's largely the debt we take on that doesn't help bring assets or additional income into our lives that causes problems. However, if the debt you have allows you to make more money with your money, that is leverage. And let me tell you—wealthy people understand leverage. Not only do they understand it, but they also use it to their advantage every chance they get.

If you have a mental block around the idea that debt is bad, it will be hard for you to embrace the concept of leverage, which is essential to building wealth.

YOUR HOME IS NOT AN ASSET

Number two, you need to understand the difference between an asset and a liability.

Years ago, the first book that changed my life was by Robert Kiyosaki, and to this day, it remains one of my core Wealthy Woman Codes. If you haven't read his books on the Cashflow Quadrant, I highly recommend them. One of the biggest lessons I took from his teachings was understanding the difference between an asset and a liability. For so many years, I was told that my house was my biggest asset—I'm sure you've heard something similar along the way.

The problem with this idea is: A) it costs me money every month, and B) I always need a place to live. Yes, there is some money tied up in your house, and when you pass away, that will be unlocked. But while you're alive and kicking, this is not really money you can access easily. Sure, some will argue that you can refinance to access it, which is true, but that just means trading the cash for another loan. You get the drift. Your house is not a wealth generator for you. The place you live is not an asset; it's a liability.

The simple way to figure out whether something is an asset or a liability is this: If it pays you, it's an asset. If it puts money in your bank account each month, week, or year, it's an asset. So, if you have a business that generates income, it's an asset. If you have investments that bring in money, it's an asset. If you have real estate that pays you, it's an asset.

Conversely, if these things are losing you money regularly, they become liabilities. For example, if you have a real estate investment that is not cash-flowing, it's a liability—get that sucker cash-flowing! If something is taking money out of your pocket each month, like a vehicle, a car payment, or a credit card payment, it's a liability.

Take a look at your balance sheet and ask yourself: What is paying you every month (an asset)? What is taking money out of your pocket (a liability)? Understanding that all your extra dollars should go toward building assets, not liabilities, will fundamentally change your life—it did for me. I now inherently understand that purchasing a new car, buying a bigger house, or indulging in new clothes are not assets; they are liabilities. Now, if they bring you joy, fantastic—but fundamentally understanding that these purchases are not assets is key. Wealthy Women spend intentional time creating assets in their portfolios and ensure their liabilities are reduced or at least bring them joy. If they take on a liability, they make sure their current assets can pay for it, or they understand the trade-off for the joy they seek. It is an intentional approach versus a consumerist one.

GENERATING INCOME AND WEALTH CREATION ARE DIFFERENT ACTIVITIES

Number three, fundamentally understanding the difference between income generation and wealth creation is key. As a coach, I can't tell you how many posts I see about the income people bring in—$100k months, $50k months, $20k months, or $10k months. It all looks very glamorous on Instagram. But what most people forget is that income generation is completely different from wealth creation; they are, in fact, very different activities. Generating more money and cash flow is one activity, but taking that cash flow and building wealth for future generations is an entirely different endeavor. You need to think about wealth creation, and it needs to be intentional. It won't happen by solely focusing on income. Income is, of course, part of it, but just creating more won't make you an automatic first-generation million-aire. What you do with your income is key, and asset building is a crucial lever in this game.

Most people think the only way to become a millionaire is to increase their income. While this is one strategy, I disagree entirely that it's the only way. You can also achieve it by taking the surplus income you have and creating assets for wealth generation. What you need to understand is that income and wealth creation are two different activities, and spending time on them separately and accordingly is necessary for driving true generational wealth.

RECEIVE WITH GRACE

Number four, giving and receiving—both are important. What's really interesting about society is that we glorify the idea of giving. And to be clear, I love giving. I think it's wonderful and an important part of the balance cycle. Give to charity, give to society, give back to the community. It is a core tenet of being wealthy. Ultimately, giving money and time reflects our values and priorities, helps us contribute to the well-being of others, and makes a positive impact on the world. But this is widely known, so I won't harp on the benefits of giving.

What I find fascinating is that we often focus less on how to receive gracefully. And I think, as women, we're not always great at this. We're told to give, give, give—give our time, give our energy, give our focus, give to our children, give to our husband, and give to our community. Very rarely do we give to ourselves, but this is of utmost importance; we have to fill our own cup first to be able to share with others. What we often forget is that receiving is part of the equation—the balance and harmony in the cycle. It's important to be able to receive gracefully. This is a key part of not blocking the potential money, abundance, and joy that could come your way. How many times have you found yourself on the receiving end of a compliment you didn't gracefully accept?

"Hi [*insert your name here*], you look beautiful today."

What is your immediate reaction? Is it, "Oh gosh, this old thing? No, no, no," and you decline the compliment? What you're telling the universe in that scenario is that you're not open to receiving. You're not open to compliments, not open to receiving more. You are blocking abundance in your life with that very response. We need to be able to show up as women and be just as comfortable receiving as we are giving. Practicing your ability to receive as gracefully as you give is essential to the flow of wealth, joy, and abundance in your life.

If you want to be the wealthiest version of yourself, it means you're going to have to let people give to you and then receive with exceptional grace.

Let me give you another example. Have you ever tried to give a gift to someone who didn't want to receive it? I took a friend out for lunch last week, and I said, "Hey, this is on me! Let me cover lunch." I hadn't seen her in a while, and I really wanted to treat her so she knew how special she was in my life despite the fact that we rarely get to see each other.

And she was like, "No, no, no, no, no, you don't have to do that." Then, she quickly pulled out her card to split the bill.

Has this scenario ever happened to you? How did it make you feel as the person who was giving? Of course, you didn't feel good. You wanted the other person to be ecstatic that you were treating them.

You wanted them to not only receive the gift with grace but to celebrate how generous you were being.

So next time you're on the receiving end of a compliment, money, a free dinner, or a coffee—remember: A Wealthy Woman always receives with grace. You, my dear, are a Wealthy Woman.

MONEY IS SIMPLY VALUE EXCHANGE, NOT A REFLECTION OF WORTH

Number five is a big one. One of the most important things you need to understand is disconnecting the idea that the money you have in your bank account is a reflection of your worth. Now, you might believe this is something you already understand. But how would you feel as a person if I took it all away tomorrow? Or if you lost your income source? We often equate our worth as individuals with what we have or accomplish. Unfortunately, this is, at its essence, the very nature of the white-picket-fence mentality and "Keeping up with the Joneses." I think, as individuals—and particularly as women—we often feel our value is tied to how much we can bring in monetarily to the house. Our ability to contribute often feels paramount. Humans, in general, feel this way. But you have to understand that our worth is not connected to the money we receive. Money is just an exchange of value. It is, in fact, a socially constructed concept meant to represent an exchange of value.

We literally could be exchanging anything—but as a society, we made up money. Paper and coins represent an energetic exchange of value. Money is simply a medium of exchange with a recognized, agreed-upon value that was adopted to make it easier for people to trade products and services with one another. Before we had money, we had bartering, where two people simply agreed on the value of the exchange. Frankly, we could be trading anything, but we invented money. And not dissimilar to bartering, our perceived value as customers can change depending largely on our needs, supply, circumstance, or location.

Let me give you an example. My uncle had an ice cream truck for many years. This was his little side business that he ran with his daughter. In the summer, they would attend concerts to sell ice cream and water at various venues. What blew me away was that they sold water bottles for $5 each at these concerts, whereas in a store, you could get a whole case for $5. It makes sense: demand was high, supply was scarce, and it was a super-hot day—there were lines for miles. Now, change that to a rainy venue: not so much—smaller lines and less demand. It wasn't the item that went down in value; sometimes it's circumstance, location, or supply. Sometimes, it depends on how much the other person values what you're selling, so you may need to change the person you are offering it to.

Money truly just represents the value that you bring to the world. If you're not making the money you want to make, it's not about whether other people value you as a person, and it's not connected to your worth as an individual. It may be the product you're offering, the room you're in, or how much reach you have. But it's not about your worth as a person. The more people who value what you have to offer, the more money that will come in. Money is just the energetic exchange of the value you're giving, but it's not connected to your worth. You are innately worthy, period.

GROWTH MINDSET OVER COMFORT EVERY TIME

I often hear people talking about a scarcity mindset, and in truth, the majority of the world does, in fact, carry this mindset in one way or another. I think it's hard to relate to a scarcity mindset—no one really wants that. But another way to talk about scarcity is just saying "comfort." We want to focus on comfort. Seriously—think about it! Everything is about comfort these days—the Snuggie, Crocs, weighted blankets, HelloFresh boxes (love me some of those)… you get the idea! Everything these days seems to be about fast comfort and convenience. People want the easy way—the comfortable, safe, secure route, minimizing turbulence and discomfort at all costs.

At the end of the day, a comfort mindset just won't make you wealthy—it will make you comfortable. If you want to be wealthy, you will have to embrace growth, which means getting really cozy with discomfort. There's nothing comfortable about taking risks, expanding, or becoming the wealthiest version of yourself. That's going to require you to grow at every turn. If your focus is comfort, it's going to be difficult to expand into the wealthiest version of yourself. But if your focus is a growth mindset—pushing yourself a little more, expanding, being uncomfortable, wrapping your arms around doing something different, getting excited by taking a risk that may or may not work out —simply taking a step when you can't see the whole picture, this will move you forward toward your wealthiest, most resilient self.

Peter Drucker, known as the "Father of Management" for his extensive studies and work in the field of business management, famously said, "Entrepreneurship is living a few years of your life like most people won't so you can live the rest of your life like most people can't." I find this quote to be true for those seeking to become intergenerational millionaires as well. There are many things along the way that others would simply turn away from in favor of comfort. But wealth generation is about holding discomfort, taking risks, and building something extraordinary.

LIFELONG LEARNING IS A NECESSARY INGREDIENT

In our society, it seems that we go to school for 12 years, sometimes a little more, and then perhaps post-secondary education. But there's a defined period where it's acceptable for your entire focus to be on learning. We take out loans for learning, and then the idea is that once the learning is "done," we're ready to launch into the world and make our great life. Society is like, "Okay! Great! You should know everything you need to know now. You're ready to roll!"

But as a Wealthy Woman, you need to embrace continuous, lifelong learning. The truth is that learning doesn't just stop after grade 12 or post-secondary. There will always be something more to know, learn, and understand. You need to start cultivating the muscle where you are comfortable asking questions, being in learning mode, and ensuring you are not the smartest person in the room. In fact, if you are in a room where you feel like you "got this" or know everything, that's a sign it's time to go on another journey of learning and find a new room. Actively deciding what new skills to acquire and what new areas to master is key. Get intentional about what you desire to learn. There is always a new skill to master, and this can be the gateway to changing your life.

New skills, new people, and new ideas can shift you in the direction of your desires. But you must be open and exercise the muscle of leaning into learning on a continuous basis. So go ahead—find a room of people who have done what you desire to do. The idea of constant lifelong learning has to be ingrained in who you are as part of your wealth-building belief system. This will help you cultivate the resilience to overcome challenges, take responsibility for learning, and lean into understanding that you, whether or not you were taught or otherwise, can take the bull by the horns and go learn something new. I promise you this will change your life.

TAX LAW IS SEXY AF

Alright, let's get real. When I tell people that they must learn about taxes to become wealthy, most of the time, their eyes glaze over, and they ask if they can somehow skip that part. Most of us would rather hire an accountant and be done with it. But did you know that according to the most recent data from the U.S. Internal Revenue Service, Americans owed over $120 billion dollars in back taxes, penalties, and interest? And for my Canadian friends, in 2022, 8.1 million Canadians owed the Canada Revenue Agency (CRA) an average of $7,426.

Okay, let's pause. That is a massive amount of money owed in back taxes between the two countries. Learning about tax law might feel boring, but it is an absolutely critical piece to understand if you want to protect your wealth. Understanding the ins and outs of taxes—how to structure yourself and your businesses—and knowing how to legally keep as much money in your pocket as possible seems like a no-brainer. Yet, many of us don't take the time to learn about taxes. It's *easier* to hire an accountant and let them deal with it.

The issue is, how do you know if they are doing it *right* for you? How can you hold them accountable? How do you ask the intelligent questions to ensure they are handling your wealth and money with care? At the end of the day, taxes are both your liability and an opportunity to protect your wealth. Yes, it might be *boring* to learn about taxes, but I highly recommend you take a course to understand them. You lead your wealth, or your wealth leads you. Understanding taxes is a key component to leading your wealth with confidence and knowledge. So say it with me: "Tax law is sexy AF."

YOUR SOUL'S MISSION WILL KEEP YOUR GAS TANK FULL

As we take this journey we call life, what I've learned is that those who are wealthy typically have a mission that's bigger than themselves. A greater purpose they serve, which is a guiding light for them in their frequency, activations, and focus. You can certainly create money just for yourself (there's no judgment here), but if it's connected to a higher purpose—a soul's mission—that is something that will keep you going. It will carry you through the hard times, the good times, and the bad times, allowing you to stay grounded and focused when things get tough.

Building a business, holding wealth, reaching more people, bringing value—it's not easy all the time. It comes with challenges and hills to climb; we all have problems—this is the human condition. But when we are plugged into a mission—a higher purpose and calling—it helps us stick with our vision, navigate new terrain, and hold onto a vision so clearly that today's evidence doesn't sway us. We all have been created in the likeness of source and given special gifts to bring to the planet. You are of infinite wisdom. To understand innately that the source, the energy source within you, the ability to create, to birth something new into the universe for the purposes of helping others— that will keep you going.

One thing that has become incredibly clear as I coach, mentor, and guide women in wealth is that no one woman has the exact same deep desires or soul downloads. While we all desire the freedom of choice, which money allows us, the missions and things we choose are very different. If you have a deep soul calling, it is meant specifically for you. That thing you keep thinking about? That deep-seated desire? The one you dream about, but which feels out of reach? Yep! That's the one. It is uniquely yours. It is your divine mission to bring it to life and achieve it for the greater good in this world during our lifetime. And when we are delivering a mission that offers great value to the planet, money will inevitably follow. So consider for yourself—what is your deep soul's mission?

EXERCISE YOUR RIGHT TO DELAY GRATIFICATION

If you know anything about the psychology of buying, you know that most people don't love the idea of delayed gratification. These days, it's all about having things immediately. Whether that's Amazon Prime (love me some overnight delivery), click-and-collect groceries, or instant access to your favorite show on Netflix, pretty much anything we want is at the click of a button. We are not excellent at exercising the muscle of delaying gratification.

Now, I am not saying that becoming a millionaire means you can't have these things. What I am saying is that one thing is very clear: Millionaires understand the long game. With such instant access to everything, we have lost the opportunity to exercise the right to delay gratification for the bigger picture. It is a muscle we must strengthen again if we want to become first-generation millionaires. Millionaires understand that time works for them in the creation of generational wealth. They understand that by foregoing something today for the bigger vision of tomorrow, they will serve themselves in the long term, and they're intentional about their decisions around gratification.

The more money you have, the less it will be about money. In fact, the more money you have, the less money becomes a restriction—you will need to start practicing discernment in your choices. The more money you have, the more choices you will have. So, it becomes incredibly important for you to understand your big-picture vision and how your choices today affect the vision of tomorrow.

Let me give you an example: A few months back, we had a surplus of money. With three young children, we've always had the desire to live on a lake. We love the water, and the idea of being able to hop onto a dock in our backyard to paddleboard or skate in the winter was very attractive. We could have purchased a big home and made this dream happen. But my big soul's mission is to create one million joyful first-generation women millionaires while creating generational wealth so my kids can live out their soul's mission without restriction. So, when we sat down, I realized that this purchase would not help us achieve that goal. It would set me back from my mission with a bigger drain on our net worth, limited additional happiness, and larger bills. The cost-benefit didn't make sense relative to what we were trying to achieve. Instead, we chose to invest that extra cash in the purchase of 16 more investment properties, which will allow us both cash flow and time freedom for years to come.

Now, I'm not saying we'll never get the house on the lake with a dock. What I'm trying to illustrate is that we made an active decision to delay gratification for the greater good of what really mattered to me. In the psychology of buying, we need to understand that we get a temporary hit of dopamine from a purchase like this, but the key word here is temporary. Assessing how much joy something will bring you relative to the greater goal of wealth alignment is an important exercise. Is this something you need right now, or is it something you can wait for while you're going after a greater, higher purpose?

MONEY IS MY EMPLOYEE

P. T. Barnum once famously said, "Money is a terrible master but an excellent servant." I couldn't agree more with this statement. One of the things that changed my life the most was really understanding that I could get money to work for me as an employee. You need to get money working for you, not the other way around. Now, I know that sounds like a funny concept, but rather than constantly going out and generating income, I could take the income I had and get it to work harder for me.

Understanding that money works for me, that it flows through me, and that it's limitless and infinite changed everything for me. Think about how you can get your money working for you so that you're not working for money. When money is not moving or working for you, this is referred to as "dead money." I want you to open your bank account—yes, right now—open the app or online portal that you have access to. Now, over the last 30 days, has everything in there been working for you? Generating income while you sleep? What parts of your bank account show "dead money?" Hint: Savings accounts can be some of the worst culprits. If you see any money that is not working for you as an employee—put it to work! Consider how you can get this money moving and working for you rather than just sitting there collecting dust.

A WOMAN DOING WELL IS EVIDENCE YOU CAN HAVE IT TOO

I would be remiss if I didn't include this as a Wealthy Woman Code. There is so much competitiveness between women, yet I want us all to anchor into the fact that we are a sisterhood. Seeing a woman who has done something amazing is evidence that it's available for you, too. This is not something that can be taken from you. We need to elevate and support one another, becoming a sisterhood that can shift the paradigm. More money in the hands of conscious women is good for the world. And the only way we're going to do that is by lifting each other up.

Women have faced many challenges that men have not. It's important for us to understand that it's not a zero-sum game: Somebody else's success does not automatically mean less for me. A woman doing well is someone to be celebrated, evidence that you can have it too. Let's lift one another up, raise our frequency, and put ourselves in that space as well.

So, let's celebrate each other, drop the jealousy, drop the envy, and deliver as a sisterhood that can change the paradigm of money on this planet.

WEALTH IS AN INSIDE JOB

While many women seek me out for financial guidance, once we dig deeper, they are looking for more than just money. They desire freedom of choice, freedom of time, and a fulfilling life mission. These are all enviable goals. But what we always end up discovering is that it's not the *things* that fill the true alignment of wealth and happiness in our hearts. Rather, money becomes the tool to design the life we desire. Ultimately, money becomes just the outcome of what you're doing. True happiness and true connectedness are found deep within; wealth and abundance are an inside job.

Knowing that Source, the universe, God—whatever you like to call it—has got you at all times and that you are divinely created to achieve any infinite desire you have is key. But fundamentally, finding joy, gratitude, and happiness within, connecting to the journey versus the outcome, will bring you true peace, alignment, joy, and freedom as a Wealthy Woman. Connecting with that internal frequency of gratitude and finding joy in what you already have will pave the way for more to enter your life in the most aligned way.

Gratitude is one of the highest frequencies available to us as humans. And when we talk about the science of energy and frequency, this is where you want to live. Having gratitude for all you have now, rather than focusing on what you desire externally, is key to shifting into a space where you feel wealthy inside before it manifests itself outwardly.

I AM CAPABLE + SAFE NO MATTER WHAT HAPPENS

I think this may just be the most important Wealthy Woman Code to download: "I am capable and safe no matter what happens." As a wealth and empowerment coach for women, I have the honor of walking alongside them on some amazing transformational journeys. Not just a journey toward more money, but toward true alignment, abundance, grace, acceptance, and freedom. It is not only an honor but also my life's soul mission. One thing I have observed is that there are moments when many women are on the precipice of diving in full steam ahead, and occasionally, they shrink back into self-doubt or fear. The "what ifs" take over, their nervous systems become dysregulated, and the next thing you know, they are second-guessing doing something they deeply desire. I bet you can relate to that at some point in your life.

But what if, for a moment, you could imagine that no matter what happens, you've got it? What if you deeply knew that no matter what —good or bad—you were safe and capable? How would that change the actions you take? This is a Wealthy Woman Belief Code I hold deeply. I believe that at the end of the day, no matter what happens, whether it works out or not, whether it goes in my favor or it doesn't, whether luck is on my side or not, it's still worth leaning in if I desire it in my life. And I know, no matter what, I am resilient, and I will figure it out for my family, my partner, my kids, and for the greater good of the mission I'm on to help other women. Understanding that you're capable no matter what happens changes everything. It makes you more... It makes you brave, bold, and ultimately, it allows you to live the best life you have in your mind's eye. So next time you're faced with a scary decision, remind yourself that you are safe and capable— and the nerves are just an exciting reminder that something amazing is on the other side of taking action.

DISCIPLINE + TENACITY IS THE GATEWAY TO FREEDOM

Let's get real. We all have days as humans when we know what we need to do but just don't have the motivation to do it. Surprised? Yes, I have those days too. You know the ones—the days where you'd rather stay in your pajamas all day and turtle from the whole wide world. But over time, I've realized that the energy of motivation is hard to sustain. We all get excited about a new venture, but slowly, over time, these things become responsibilities, and that can feel heavy. But I strongly believe, to my core, that discipline is the key to freedom. It's on the days when I know what to do but don't do it that guilt and frustration start to seep in. Next thing you know, I'm beating myself up and looking in the freezer for a tub of ice cream—you feel me? But cultivating discipline means taking the steps even when we don't feel like it. Discipline is what can reduce our anxiety, change our life into what we desire, and allow us to take action even without motivation. This Wealthy Woman Code has allowed me to ride the highs and lows of motivation by creating habits of discipline and tenacity, which turn actions into reality over time. Downloading this code will allow magic to enter your life.

These Wealthy Woman Codes I've shared with you continue to evolve throughout my life. But they are fundamental ideas and beliefs that form the basis of all my decisions and actions. And as you know, beliefs are incredibly important—it's just science. While I'll continue to add to these as I spiral higher in my journey, these are some I had to embrace to break through to becoming a joyful first-generation woman millionaire and to change my life for the better. I believe if you look at these, you'll find ways to embody them in your life, too, so you can become the wealthiest version of yourself and achieve the goals you have in your mind's eye, no matter what they are.

As you reflect on these codes, I want you to consider what your own divine soul's mission is. I guarantee that if you sit down and share your innermost desires with someone, theirs will be different from yours. There are moments when I think about how I don't want to be lying on my deathbed with my divine downloads still in me. I want to get them out into the universe. The universe needs more Wealthy Women—women who believe in themselves so much that they're willing to be bold, brave, and live as the wealthiest version of themselves.

Money is just a tool. Getting clear on what it is you want to design for your life and what brings you joy is of utmost importance. The Wealthy Woman Belief Codes are a start, but ultimately, what you're trying to design and your deep desires are what matter most. Having the desire for money is one thing, but what you're going to do with it and why is another piece to unpack.

REFLECTION QUESTIONS

Again, grab that notebook and journal to keep your money reflections close. I promise after you activate and embody through reading this book, you will want to reflect and contemplate all your ideas as you rise to the Wealthy Woman you are.

1. Which Wealthy Woman Codes did I resonate with the most? Why?

_____

_____

_____

_____

2. Which Wealthy Woman Codes challenged my core beliefs the most? Why?

_____

_____

_____

_____

3. Which Wealthy Woman Code would I like to adopt and activate in my life? How will I do this?

_____

_____

_____

_____

4. What do I think about when I hear the word "debt?" Why? Is there something I need to unravel around the idea of debt to embrace the idea of leverage? If so, what is it I need to redefine?

_____

_____

_____

_____

5. What are my key liabilities? What are my key assets? Would I like to build more assets? If so, which ones do I desire to explore?

_____

_____

_____

_____

6. Do I actively build wealth now? Why or why not? What could I do differently to build my wealth so money becomes my employee?

_____

_____

_____

_____

7. Do I regularly choose a growth mindset or a comfort mindset? Why or why not? What mindset do I desire? How can I make small changes to shift in that direction?

_____

_____

_____

_____

8. If money wasn't a restriction in my life, what would I do with my time?

_____

_____

_____

_____

9. What do I believe is my soul's mission? How can I take steps to bring my soul's mission forward and activate value for the world?

_____

_____

_____

_____

10. What is the big vision for my life that I carry in my heart?

_____

_____

_____

_____

ACTIVATIONS

This chapter has so many options for activations, so if something else calls you, feel free to do it! Here are some suggestions that will help you embody the Wealthy Woman Codes! Choose at least two to do this week:

1. Publicly recognize and celebrate a woman who is accomplishing what you desire to do! Celebrate her with all the love, grace, and praise in your heart. An easy way to do this is on social media or in a public forum.

2. Grab your net worth statement and review which items are assets and which are liabilities. Are there any shifts you would like to make? If so, which one and how will you activate these shifts?

3. Engage in lifelong learning by finding a coach, mentor, or course to teach you something new that will support your soul's mission. Perhaps it's taxes, wealth, social media, marketing, or business! Anything you desire that will help you move forward.

4. Find a woman who is doing what you desire to be doing and reach out for a discussion! Take this moment of connection and learning as evidence that you can do it, too.

5. Join the private Quantum Femme Wealth: Joyful First Generation Millionaire Money Talk! Facebook group and introduce yourself. Share your deepest desires as you join the ride to become a joyful, first-generational millionaire.

Now that we've got our heads around the basic science of the quantum energetics of money and understand that money is just a reflection of the value we create, the next chapter will dive into how to find the unique lifestyle that brings you joy and set it to find practical surplus and abundance in your life.

CHAPTER 5

Lifestyle Alignment

*"Money is only a tool. It will take you wherever you wish
but not replace you as the driver."*
–Ayn Rand

With a background in marketing, one of the things that fascinates me is branding and buying behavior. Specifically, the idea that how we position something in the mind of a consumer can influence whether they like it, buy it, or even pay more or less for it. There is an entire discipline in marketing dedicated to buyer behavior—where psychology meets creativity. Through my education in marketing, I came to understand that what I buy offers me a temporary dopamine hit and that branding, in its essence, is an effort to make me prefer one product over another.

Branding, at its core, is the process of creating a unique identity and image for a company or product in the minds of consumers. Effective branding helps establish a connection with customers, communicating the values and qualities of the brand, which either resonates with the consumer or validates who they are as a person. And goodness, don't we all love to stand for something and be validated!

In my consumer behavior class at university, I learned that brand-name companies often manufacture items for no-name brands. The items are virtually identical, yet the one with a brand can charge significantly more. If you don't believe me, next time you're buying Advil, check the back of the no-name brand. Compare the ingredients and manufacturers—you'll be surprised to see there's little to no difference.

So, what makes us choose one item over another? Ultimately, it's our beliefs about who we are and how a purchase either aligns with or validates our identity.

Don't get me wrong—there are excellent examples of companies and products with beautiful brands and incredible craftsmanship, like a locally handcrafted soap or an artisan-crafted table made from hand-logged wood. For those, the value exchange is entirely appropriate. But we must ask ourselves, does this item genuinely bring joy, or is it just a temporary dopamine hit validating something we can't validate within ourselves? If it brings true joy, great. If not, it's time to pause and reflect.

Don't even get me started on pricing theory. If something is more expensive, we tend to believe it has more value, whereas if it's cheaper, we assume it has less value. Understanding these concepts has fundamentally changed how I view purchasing products and services.

Just being aware that buying gives us a temporary dopamine hit—so it only feels good temporarily—has made me pause before making purchases. I now ask myself these questions: *Will this truly bring me joy? Is this something that will offer long-term happiness, or am I seeking external validation? Is this aligned with my long-term goals, or is it just a quick fix?*

This awareness has fundamentally shifted me from being an external consumer to a creator of my own aligned happiness, freedom, and joy. It's allowed me to make intentional purchases that bring more gratitude and fulfillment, and I'm happy to offer the energetic exchange of money for those things.

Many of us get trapped in the white-picket-fence mentality or try to "keep up with the Joneses" without stopping to consider how much joy, freedom, or happiness those things actually bring. This phenomenon is referred to as lifestyle inflation or lifestyle creep. Lifestyle creep occurs when an individual's spending increases as their income rises. Have you ever noticed that when someone's income rises, their expenses often rise, too? They suddenly have a bigger house and a fancier car and take more luxurious vacations. In this scenario, as income increases, so do expenses and obligations—often disproportionately—leading to additional stress and worry, the opposite of the joy and freedom they likely desired.

So why is being aware of lifestyle creep so important? Why is it essential to ensure our financial decisions are aligned with our true desires in a conscious, intentional way? Because many believe that the only path to wealth is through increasing income. But if most people fall victim to lifestyle creep, we're missing a key part of the wealth equation—surplus. If we continually increase our expenses as income rises, we'll never reach a surplus. To generate wealth, we must find surplus and redirect it to wealth-creation activities while simultaneously creating a lifestyle that brings joy and happiness.

As women, if we want to become the first generation of joyful millionaires, we must first think about what truly matters to us instead of falling prey to lifestyle creep in an attempt to keep up with the Joneses.

Have you ever noticed one of the ongoing headlines about Warren Buffett is that he still lives in the same old house he's always lived in? The billionaire is famously frugal. In fact, the 92-year-old has lived in the same modest home in Omaha, Nebraska, for 65 years.

He purchased it in 1958 for $31,500, which is about $329,000 in today's dollars. Ever wondered why? When asked this question by the BBC, Buffett explained, "I'm happy there. I would move if I thought I'd be happier someplace else. But this house does just fine." He added, "I'm warm in the winter, cool in the summer, and it's very convenient for me. I couldn't imagine having a better house."

What Warren reveals in this answer is that despite his wealth, he's content where he is because he knows what brings him joy—and a bigger, fancier house isn't it. He also reveals that if something brought him more happiness, he wouldn't hesitate to move. Buffett seems more excited by investing in companies that build the value of humanity and having a surplus to build even more financial freedom. He made a conscious decision to say no to lifestyle creep and yes to wealth-building through his investments.

That's not to say I don't understand the pressure we face to increase our lifestyle. I am not immune. Do you remember the bigger house with the dock I said no to? The media and society don't help women with this either. We're constantly bombarded with images of wealth as external things we acquire: fancy cars, designer clothes, constant travel, private jets, and bigger houses. In fact, many of these items are actually depreciating assets that cost money each month and decrease in value over time—not exactly a wealth-building strategy.

If you want to become a millionaire, you'll need to find balance in your lifestyle. You'll need to be absolutely clear on what truly brings you happiness and joy and practice discernment to avoid falling into the trap of the white-picket-fence mentality or lifestyle creep.

You'll need to dig deep and connect with what's most important to you. You must, in fact, get to a place where you can live on less than you make so that you can use the surplus intentionally to create wealth and get your money working for you. This will enable you to build the time, freedom, and freedom of choice you desire. It is what you do with your time and your surplus that will pave the road to becoming the first millionaire in your family. You will need to transcend the white-picket-fence narrative and build your own path forward.

Dave Ramsay conducted the largest study of millionaires in the USA, interviewing over 10,000 of them. This study revealed some key habits that are unique to millionaires. I've selected a few key findings to bolster our discussion here:

1. Millionaires live on less than they make—yes, here's that surplus again! They don't rely on credit cards or buy things they can't afford. While budgeting may seem boring, it's really about creating an intentional plan.

2. On average, millionaires drive four-year-old cars. Millionaires understand that cars are a depreciating asset and one of the worst things to spend money on. Don't get me wrong, you need a car to get from place to place, but the truth is, they are a terrible waste of money. So, find something practical and understand how you can write off the expense through your business, but don't make the mistake of thinking a fancy car will get you ahead from a wealth perspective.

3. Millionaires believe deeply that they are in control of their financial destiny. A staggering 97% of millionaires believe they control their financial destiny. Regardless of how they grew up, they believe they have control, autonomy, and agency over their money. They believe they get to tell it where it needs to go. Lastly, they are intentional about their money. They create a budget and make a plan.

Lifestyle alignment is all about intentional living while creating space to build wealth with your surplus. At the core of keeping up with the Joneses is fear of missing out and dissatisfaction. We believe that if we have the things others have, it will make us happy. However, buyer psychology suggests the opposite; the purchase provides a short-term dopamine hit, but sustained dopamine is hard to come by through external things. Dopamine is the pleasure chemical, and while it feels good when released, it's only temporary when tied to external purchases.

At the end of the day, you've got to run your own race. You've got to determine the rules of your game for joy, freedom, and happiness—and protect them ruthlessly.

So, what brings you true joy? Be thoughtful about this because the most joyous things are likely independent of money. Money is nice, and of course, it enables us to access things, experiences, and time freedom. But joy is a very different frequency. Why chase others who you don't even really like or care about?

Spending time reflecting on what brings you deep joy and happiness is crucial because, as more money comes in, it will amplify who you already are. If you are a good person, more money will mean you do more good. If you are an unhappy person, it will likely bring more unhappiness. If you're already happy, it'll make you even happier. Understanding what brings you true happiness in each area of your life is a key step in directing your money where it needs to go. You need to determine who you are today and what really brings you joy. Making the decision to run your own race and practicing clarity and discernment will pave the way for you to rise as your wealthiest self.

You will have to transcend the white-picket-fence narrative and dive deep into your inner knowing. Drop out of your head, ignore the social media bombardment, and tune into your body. What does your heart tell you?

On a personal note, I can tell you that a homemade bun from my mother-in-law, fresh out of the oven, brings me as much joy today as it did when I had no money. The warmth of sunshine on my skin on a summer's day, the smell of rain after a storm, the sound of crickets at night with the window cracked open—all bring me immense joy. Watching my family laugh around the dinner table, seeing my son dunk a basketball and celebrate, or watching my kids explore bugs in the dirt—these are sacred moments. A warm bowl of soup my husband makes when I'm not feeling well or the thrill of catching my first wave of the day in the ocean—these are the things I hold dear, money or no money.

Of course, I have goals, dreams, and desires that are not always wealth-oriented—they are more joy-oriented. And that's okay, too. It's about having the intentional awareness that your actions and purchases come from a place of joy, not necessarily wealth-building, and that these decisions are made with educated awareness and conscious intent. For example, I'd love to have a property where my family can escape—a sunny location with surf nearby, beautiful big windows overlooking the ocean, and a pool where my kids can do cannonballs. I can already see it in my mind's eye. That's not a wealth-building exercise, but as I get clearer on what truly brings me joy, like travel, being with my family, surfing, and putting my toes in the sand, this becomes something I will put on a vision board and make happen. And of course, it will require money, but without thoughtful reflection on what truly brings me joy, I couldn't have become clear on this purchase, which will bring me abundance in a different way.

Many women dream of complete time freedom and freedom of choice. What a beautiful dream: to laze in the sun, soak in vitamin D, sip green juice, hear the waves crashing, watch children playing in the sand, and do afternoon yoga. Nowhere to be, nothing to worry about —just enjoying the moment. Meanwhile, a business runs effortlessly in the background, generating $50,000 or $100,000 a month with minimal oversight—except for the parts you love, intentionally designed to keep you engaged. Doesn't that sound delightful?

I've actually helped women get to this exact place. And do you know what shows up then? "I feel bored. I don't have a purpose. I'm not sure what to do with my time, energy, and money." At the end of the day, you need to be thoughtful about what you want at all levels. The more money that comes in, the clearer you need to be on what matters. More money means more decisions. The interesting thing about not having money is that it acts as a restrictor—you have fewer options. The more money you have, the more options you have, but you still have to choose.

So, you need to figure out exactly what matters to you. What is the lifestyle alignment you're trying to create? What is it you really want? If you have money but lack gratitude for the life you've built, what's the point? If we're not in awe of our lives each day for the money we have, again, what's the point?

Money simply amplifies who you already are, and the key is that you don't have to wait for money to discover what brings you joy. You can find that today, and then the money will flow in. You can reflect intentionally on what is important for your lifestyle at any stage. This is crucial to shifting toward your happiest, most joyous, wealthiest self. And this needs to be an ongoing exercise. As we've already discovered, we are energy, and our intentions change. We evolve, and our priorities shift. Being intentional about revisiting your ultimate desires and checking in regularly with your life alignment is important. If you're embracing growth, your desires will evolve and change over time. This isn't a "set it and forget it" exercise. I recommend checking in at least once or twice a year. It's always good to pivot and tweak your vision, goals, and actions to maintain alignment as you go.

Aligning your energy and emotions with the joy you truly desire will allow you to direct the money you have toward the life you want to create. This isn't something you wait to do; you do it now, regardless of where you are in your journey. I promise you, by the time the money comes and you reach the moment you've always dreamed of, it won't be the big deal you thought it would be. By that point, you've already built a beautiful life, and the money is just the cherry on top. Celebrate with gratitude along the way because this frequency will bring in more joy, more abundance, more freedom, more bravery, and ultimately, the wealthiest version of yourself. Tap into the abundance that's already present in your life.

CLEARING OUT

As energetic beings, we only have so much energy to create the life we desire. We must be intentional about our lifestyle alignment, getting super clear on what brings us joy and happiness, and equally intentional about removing things that drain our energy and don't contribute to the life we want. Many people can easily imagine what they want, but they aren't clear on what they're willing to sacrifice or what work they're willing to put in to get to that desired space. I remember a time in my life when I was crying, head in hands. I was drowning in debt, deeply unhappy in my marriage, and felt like I was living someone else's life. So much energy was going out the door just to get through the day, let alone to make big decisions and take big risks. My focus became just getting through the day with a level of comfort—until I was ready to make the incredibly difficult decision to choose a different life.

You simply can't plant a new garden if there's already one completely full. You have to decide what to pull out and cull, so to speak, to till the garden. Otherwise, it will just crowd out the new plants. If you desire a truly wealthy, happy, and free life, you need to get real about where you are today and what needs to change to make space for creating your ultimate life. You will likely have to pull some weeds, decide what plants are new, till the soil, and make space for something new. You need to be clear on the work you're willing to put in, what you need to let go of, and what skills you might need to learn to get there. You probably need to plant some new seeds, give them time, water them, let them get some sun, and so on. If you are in a position where a lot of energy is going out the door because key areas of your life are not in order, you need to take note. This does not leave enough energy for you to make the important decisions you need to make in your life. To create wealth, you need to be able to hold more, to expand, to see opportunities, and to trust yourself to lean into them. You need to ensure that your garden is ready for growth and free of weeds.

Creating wealth takes intention. It requires energy, focus, and ruthless discernment for the greater good of what you're trying to create. If you're not taking care of your physical, intellectual, emotional, and spiritual well-being, there won't be space to create this alternate life with intention. Lifestyle alignment is about getting crystal clear on what brings you joy but also being very real about what you need to remove from your life. Reflect on what's working for you, what's not working, what skills you need to learn, what beliefs you need to rewire, what actions you need to take, and what fears you need to face. At the end of the day, you must choose to be brave enough to make these choices, to remove what needs to be removed, and to put in the work on the areas you want to call into your life. It is truly a choice—a choice to either stay comfortable or grow into the new wealthy version that is your divine right.

Statisticians have calculated the odds that you specifically were born as a human to walk this lovely round ball we call earth and had the chance at life—yes, I am talking to you in all your unique, sexy, limited edition-ness! So let me take a moment to blow your mind—the odds that you were born with a chance at life, reading this book about how to squeeze the joy out of it with every last drop of it—one in four hundred quadrillion. You've literally won the proverbial lottery just by existing. So now is the time to use this gift to build the life you desire. You must be able to create energetic space and lifestyle alignment, as money will simply amplify what you already have. The foundation needs to be in order. Money is simply a tool and an amplifier of the life you've already created. If you're in a terrible relationship or an unhappy job, money will not make it better. It's not the solution; it will just amplify what you've already got. Getting your life in order, creating energetic space, and flexing your muscles of discernment and focus to trust your decisions are absolutely key. Once you've cleared some space and are laser-focused on what matters to you—creating life in alignment with intention—it's time to look more practically at how you can receive new abundance in your life.

PRIORITIES, NOT BALANCE

As you seek to align your lifestyle, it can be helpful to consider the core areas of your life: health, finances, personal growth, family, income generation, pleasure, relationships, and spirituality. Reflecting on these core areas will help you understand your desires and the elements of joy while highlighting areas that might need some work. As mentioned, this is an ongoing process.

Where I see women get tripped up is the desire to have everything in balance. I don't know about you, but finding balance in my life can be difficult at times, as demands and responsibilities are always piling up. As women, we are often pulled in many different directions at once. The pressure to be a good mom, wife, friend, daughter, boss, entrepreneur—it can feel like a lot. Most high-performing women often feel fried, burnt out, and, frankly, unhappy with their perfor-mance in many areas of life. Here is a key lesson in lifestyle alignment that changed my life: I stopped focusing on "doing it all" and redefined what *all* means to me. I can "have it all," but I also get to define what *all* is.

Rather than looking at your life and trying to juggle everything, consider this: If everything were falling apart around you, and you were holding massive discomfort due to expansion or demands in your life, which parts of your life would you hold sacred? Which areas are most important? Let's look at that list of life areas again: health, finances, personal growth, family, income generation, pleasure, relationships, and spirituality. Now, pick two that you will protect no matter what, come hell or high water. It's inevitable that the proverbial "you know what" will hit the fan now and again—we are, after all, human. Problems are part of living. So when this happens, as it will, I want you to pre-meditate for yourself which two areas of your life you will protect and give yourself the grace to let the rest go, at least temporarily. Creating a plan of your core priorities will help you not only give yourself grace but also free up energetic space to continue focusing on your greater goal of building the life you desire in alignment. This will begin to shift freedom internally for yourself.

In the next chapter, we'll explore joyful income generation for surplus, both energetically and practically, so you can call in your best life. Joyful income generation is key to finding surplus, wealth creation, and ultimately using money to build the life of your dreams.

REFLECTION QUESTIONS

Grab your sacred reflection journal and contemplate the following questions for yourself:

1. Have you ever felt pressure to keep up with the Joneses or achieve the white-picket-fence mentality? If so, when? How has your perspective changed after reading this chapter?

_____

_____

_____

_____

2. Have you ever experienced lifestyle creep? If so, when and how did this happen? How has your perspective changed with greater awareness of the concept?

_____

_____

_____

_____

3. Have you ever observed someone else experiencing lifestyle creep? How did you know it was this phenomenon?

_____

_____

_____

_____

4. Is there anything you need to remove from your life to allow your desires to fully come in? Be honest with yourself here.

_____

_____

_____

_____

5. What are the two core areas of your life you will protect at all costs? In other words, out of wealth, health, family, relationships, spirituality, friendship, and income generation, what are the ones you will prioritize no matter what? What would you rate each area of your life now

out of 10? What would make it a 10? Use the "Wheel of Wealth" below to reflect on each area. Once you have the priorities set, you can reflect on whether you are acting in alignment with those focuses in your money decisions and daily actions.

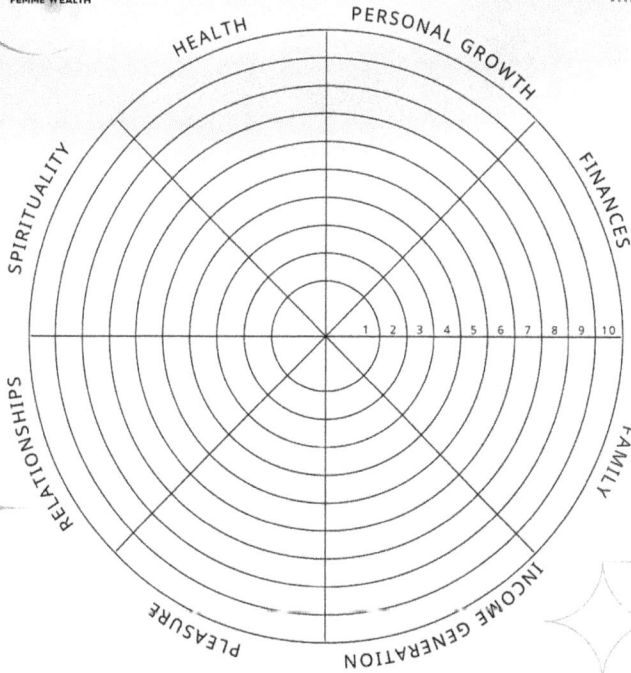

Priority categories

Notes

ACTIVATIONS

1. Write out a list of 100 things that bring you deep joy and happiness.
2. Go to www.quantumfemmewealth.com and join our email list for tips and tricks for lifestyle alignment and wealth.

CHAPTER 6

Joyful Income Generation for Surplus

*"Doing well has little to do with how smart you are
and a lot to do with how you behave."*
–Morgan Housel

When I was about eight years old, I vividly remember playing in the front yard with some friends who lived in a cul-de-sac near us. It was a really warm summer day, and of course, we had our music blaring as we practiced gymnastics on the lawn, trying to impress each other with our skills. I was wearing my best little gymnast suit, trying to perfect my cartwheel into a round-off since flips were beyond my ability.

As I landed the round-off, I noticed something shiny out of the corner of my eye. It was a little penny. I grabbed it and proudly announced to my friends, "Find a penny, pick it up, and all day long, you'll have good luck!" In my effort to show off, I took the penny and, without thinking, threw it toward the trash can. For the life of me, I can't remember why I did this. Maybe it was the excitement of the music, or maybe it was just a reflex, a bit of a celebratory moment. I'm still not sure. However, while I was celebrating, my father was watching as he puttered in the garden in the background. He was not happy. He had seen that penny fly from my hands straight into the trash. The music switched off, and without explanation, he immediately sent all my friends home. There I was, standing in my little gym suit, utterly confused.

"Dad, why did you send all my friends home?" I asked.

He responded sternly, "Jasmine, come sit with me."

He guided me to the front steps, and I sat as he explained that throwing away a penny was disrespectful to money. He said we must always appreciate and care for money when it comes to us. As a result, I was grounded for the rest of the day.

At the time, the grounding felt a little harsh. I mean, really? Grounded for throwing out a penny? In hindsight, I can see my father was trying to teach me a valuable lesson about our relationship with money and how gratitude is tied to the flow of abundance. If I couldn't respect a penny, how could the universe ever deliver more riches to me?

I'm sure you have stories about money too and your relationship with it. Stories that are equally interesting. But have you ever really stopped to think? You are indeed in a relationship with money. And what do we all want in relationships? Most people desire healthy, loving, and trusting companions. They want relationships that contribute to a strong, lasting bond where each person feels loved and cherished.

Some of the things most people desire in relationships are:

1. **Trust.** They want trust. They want a strong foundation, ensuring both partners feel secure and confident and have each other's backs.
2. **Open Communication.** They want honest and respectful communication that helps partners understand each other's needs, resolve conflicts, and build deeper connections. They want to be listened to, heard, and acknowledged.

3. **Respect.** They want mutual respect and understanding of individuality, differences, and boundaries.

4. **Mutual Love and Affection.** They want expressions of love, both physical and emotional. They want to feel valued and supported—emotionally, mentally, and financially—during good times and bad.

5. **Commitment.** They want to know there's a commitment to each other's well-being and long-term alignment in their goals.

6. **Compatibility.** They want shared values, interests, and life goals to help align their paths and create harmonious relationships.

7. **Closeness and Intimacy.** Beyond physical intimacy, they want emotional closeness and vulnerability to create a deeper bond.

8. **Compromise.** They want a willingness to find a middle ground, make sacrifices for the benefit of the relationship, and show dedication and flexibility.

9. **Fun and Adventure.** They want to enjoy each other's company, share humor, and have fun, keeping the relationship vibrant and joyful.

10. **To Feel Heard and Understood.** Feeling heard, seen, acknowledged, and understood enriches relationships to new levels.

While the list could go on, these elements contribute to a happy relationship where both partners feel loved, respected, and fulfilled, promoting long-term happiness and stability. Guess what? You are in a relationship with money, and money wants these things, too. Money wants you to appreciate every dollar that flows into your accounts. It wants you to open the mail and acknowledge how much is coming in and going out. It wants you to be grateful for the bills that keep the lights on and for the things you have intentionally purchased. Money wants to make sure you trust it and that it trusts you. Ask yourself, do you have a fundamental trust issue with money? Maybe it's not working because you don't trust it. Money wants you to have love, affection, and appreciation. It wants to know you're compatible with each other. Money wants to know you've got each other's backs, that you're willing to compromise, and that there's ultimate trust. Most importantly, money wants to go where it's fun. It wants to be understood and to experience levity and playfulness every day. Money wants to feel good around you just as much as you want to feel good with money.

Yesterday, I walked around my house, acknowledging all the elements of money and abundance that I had previously overlooked. In my life, I've noticed that when I truly appreciate and acknowledge the abundance flowing in, it actually amplifies. One thing I challenge you to consider is: Where is the money and abundance flowing in your life that you haven't noticed before? Start paying attention. Be more intentional. Look for it. Be grateful for the money you see. Maybe you find a penny on the driveway, or a dime or a quarter like I did. But more likely, you might find something like unexpected gift cards, a refund, or maybe someone buying you a coffee. All of this is an example of respecting money, acknowledging it, and building a strong relationship with it.

Money wants to be received with joy and happiness! Like greeting your partner at the door after a long day at the office. We must get exceptionally good at receiving money joyfully, gratefully, gracefully, and celebrating it in all forms as it comes into our lives. Otherwise, we choke out the flow of money and tarnish the relationship. If you start practicing being in a healthy relationship with money, giving gratitude for what it adds to your life, the universe and money will respond in a positive, amplified way.

When we talk about joyful income generation, the first step is getting real about your relationship with money. If you were to describe your relationship with money today, are you excited when it flows in? Do you open your mail right away to see what money is offering? Do you honor and give thanks for the bills that come in, acknowledging that they bring forth something valuable in your life in exchange for that money? Do you celebrate the simplest forms of money flowing in, such as an unexpected refund from your insurance company or a discount on your favorite snack? Practicing awareness, understanding, and celebrating money in your life are all signals to money that it is in the right place, in a relationship with you!

YOUR ENERGETIC SET POINT

My first job was at a marketing agency in Toronto, an experiential marketing agency that worked for brands like L'Oréal, Maybelline, Garnier, Redken, and Kraft, to name just a few. Coming out of college, I thought I had made it big time with my annual salary just a hair over $40,000. I remember feeling grateful for the consistent income landing in my bank account every two weeks. I felt like I had finally made it and that all those student loans were completely worth it. The funny thing was, as the years went on, I noticed that 2% to 3% raises were just enough to keep me satisfied. I felt like I was contributing, but in the end, it was just enough to keep me around. Despite desiring more, why was it that I would just settle for the same? I wasn't contributing less—I was continuing to bring more value every year at similar rates. That's when I started learning about something called the "energetic money set point."

Your energetic money set point is the amount of money you feel comfortable making—neither too much nor too little. Think of it like a thermostat, your "wealth thermostat," if you will. Just like the thermostat in your home, where the air conditioner kicks on if it gets too hot and the furnace kicks on if it gets too cold, your wealth thermostat works the same way.

In fact, your subconscious mind will keep you within your money set point because that's your safe zone, where you feel most comfortable. If you try to exceed this energetic money set point, you'll find yourself sabotaging your efforts as you try to move forward. Conversely, if you dip below your energetic set point, you might start feeling anxious and worried, prompting you to take action to increase your money back to that level. For example, if you lose your job or no longer have an income stream, you might start to panic and take steps to recover financially.

Your energetic money set point is ultimately the amount of money your body, heart, mind, and soul feel comfortable making—it's the amount you return to again and again. It becomes a sort of glass ceiling. It's the amount your nervous system feels good about making, and it might seem silly, but when you exceed this amount, you start to feel unsafe. When you go below it, you also feel unsafe.

If you're curious about what your energetic set point is, try this exercise: Explore how much per hour you're comfortable charging. For example, how does $20 an hour feel? What about $100? $200 per hour? $300 per hour? $400? $500 per hour? What about $750? $1,500? $3,000? $10,000? Keep going. Where did you start to feel uncomfortable? Where did you start to think, *No, that would be a rip-off*? On the other hand, where did you feel uncomfortable with it being too low? Where did you start to question whether it was appropriate to charge that amount?

Maybe you're making $4,000 per month right now. You might be thinking, *Of course, I'd be okay with $20,000 if that amount started flowing in*. But unconsciously, something is holding you back because the truth is, you're making $4,000, not $20,000. Ultimately, you probably have some unconscious blocks that you need to clear out that are holding you back.

You may have heard people say before, *Something is holding me back. Why am I stuck at this income level?* It's because your subconscious money mind doesn't think it's safe for you to go to the next level. So, how do you know if you're unconsciously hitting your proverbial energetic money set point or glass ceiling? Tune into your body. When you think about your next money goal, maybe going from $100,000 to $200,000 per year, does it feel easy, normal, seamless? Or do you start to feel tension in your body? If you detect discomfort, tightness, or nerves, that's your body telling you that you're hitting your energetic set point, which could be choking out your potential to receive more.

Sometimes, the discomfort isn't about the number itself but what you have to do to get there. For example, it might mean asking for a raise, changing jobs, growing your audience, learning a new skill, or becoming a better salesperson. I see many women in my coaching business who don't like being visible—they find it uncomfortable to be seen on social media or elsewhere. This is an example of an energetic set point that limits your ability to reach more people and, therefore, limits your income.

Tuning into your intuition and understanding what your body is telling you can help you uncover the nuances that might be holding you back. These signals can inform your next steps. They could be things like avoiding certain tasks, not wanting to move forward in a particular area, or feeling discomfort. These are all examples of energetic money set points or glass ceilings that you'll need to consider. These clues will help you understand the steps you need to take to expand your money energetic set point. Once you gain clarity about your current money energetic set point, you can begin to work on expanding your capacity to receive more.

This process might involve addressing limiting beliefs about your ability to manage money, increasing the consistency of your income generation, and working on nervous system regulation and rewiring to help you break through. This could look like reviewing your money beliefs, exercising your capacity for risk, or committing to the work required to achieve your desires. At the end of the day, it's time to receive with joy.

Welcome this new era of joyful income generation into your life, and practice holding expansion and capacity with grace. My deep truth is that I don't believe you need to make seven figures a year to become a generational millionaire, but you do need to consider your cash flow and how you'll generate joyful income consistently now and in the future. You also need to practice receiving more and asking for more so that you can maximize your value exchange.

As you seek to expand your income generation joyfully, there are practical levers you can pull to accelerate and grow your wealth. Each of these levers can help you collapse time and increase your income. Depending on where you are in your wealth journey, some or all of these strategies may resonate. I encourage you to reflect on where you are today and consider which of these approaches might make the most sense for you now. As your journey to building more wealth continues, you may revisit this list and try something new to further increase your income. Let's dive into some of these options:

1. **Ask for a Raise**. According to a Robert Half survey in Canada, women are less likely to ask for a raise than their male counterparts—56% of women versus 64% of men. For my American friends, a CNBC survey revealed that while men and women are equally likely to ask for a raise, men are more likely to receive one—52% of women who ask receive it, compared to 59% of men. While the gap in equity is something we still need to address, the key takeaway is that if you take action and ask for a raise, you have a 50% chance of getting one. As an investment, those odds sound pretty good to me. So go ahead and ask. And if you don't get what you want, remember, it doesn't mean anything about your worth. If someone doesn't see the value you bring, it doesn't mean you don't have value—perhaps you're just in the wrong room.

2. **Knock on Some Doors for Something New**. If you're not getting what you want in your current role, a Wealthy Woman knows how to pivot. She understands that if she doesn't receive the raise or promotion she desires, it's just time for something new. So, maybe you're in a job that is "okay," or you're in the so-called "golden handcuffs"—good, comfortable, decent money, but not your ideal way to generate income. It's time to explore alternatives and become the wealthiest version of yourself. One way to feel powerful again is simply to have options, and searching for a new job is a numbers game. The more doors you knock on, the more chances you have of something opening—it's just math. The key is, if you want something new, get out of your head, dust off your résumé, and do the work. Having options puts the ball back in your court. According to the

Atlanta Federal Reserve Bank wage growth tracker, wage gains favor job switchers over those who stay put. While this might paint a dismal picture of loyalty to your current employer, it offers valuable insight for you when it's time to move. If you're not getting the money you want for your time and energy, there could be plenty of opportunities to increase your income by exploring alternatives. Remember, it's just a numbers game—send out those résumés and let the universe do the rest. Personally, I've always managed to increase my income by transitioning roles. It's a great way to boost your income quickly, but you must be willing to do the work, be vulnerable, knock on doors, and stay open to receiving something new.

3. **Negotiate a Higher Salary**. Once you've knocked on some doors, it's inevitable that something will open, and an offer will land in your hands. When that happens, you must show up as the Wealthy Woman you are. The gender pay gap in the U.S. is sometimes linked to differences in how women and men approach salary negotiations. According to a Pew Research Center survey, most U.S. workers who are not self-employed say they did not ask for higher pay than what was initially offered the last time they were hired for a job. Men are slightly more likely than women (32% versus 28%) to ask for more than what was offered. But a Wealthy Woman knows that to receive her highest income, she must be unafraid to ask for it. So, when that offer lands in your hands, it's time to be brave—ask for more. The response will tell you whether or not to accept the position.

4. **Learn a New Skill**. If you're feeling stuck or stagnant, it might be time to learn a new skill. Ongoing learning is key to becoming the wealthiest version of yourself, and recognizing when it's time to level up is crucial. If you're a bit lost or know exactly where you want to go, chances are you'll need to invest energy into learning something new. Hire a coach, attend a professional development class, or

take a course—whatever it takes. Ask yourself: Where do I need more confidence? What do I need to learn to become the best version of myself? Is there something I tend to delegate that I should really know more about? Lean into learning about areas that scare you a little. Many women I talk to want to learn about investing, but few take a course or dive in with questions—they just hand it off to a financial advisor. If you're in a relationship with money, you need to know exactly where it's going and how it's getting there. Don't let someone else take fees without being confident that you know exactly what's happening and why and that you truly want to pay them for their services.

5. **Start a Business**. As you continue to develop your skills, you might find yourself in a position to offer something of value to the world. As a Wealthy Woman, there comes a moment when you realize that you have only so many hours in the day. As an employee, there are only so many hours you can leverage. This is where you might consider starting your own business or purchasing one to run. In this option, you can either be self-employed or a business owner. In either case, I encourage you to consider how best to leverage your time and skills to build the business most effectively. Creating a solid business can be a great source of joyful income generation and diversification, as well as a valuable asset for your portfolio. Business owners have a system where other people work for them. Consider Henry Ford, who surrounded himself with smart people who knew the answers, allowing him to concentrate on new ideas. This is where you start to think about how to leverage other people's time. Business owners understand that while they only have so many hours in the day, hiring others allows them to expand those hours exponentially. The biggest advantage of buying an existing business is that you inherit an existing blueprint, including an established customer base, defined operating expenses, and fully trained

employees. By adding value to technology and improving efficiency, you can increase the company's value relatively quickly. On the other hand, simply starting a small online business offers the opportunity for an additional income stream and helps reduce reliance on a single source of funds.

6. **Review Your Pricing Strategy**. If you are already a business owner, unlike an employee asking for a raise, you may need to review your pricing strategy. Business owners should regularly review their pricing strategies to ensure alignment with their goals, market conditions, and competitive landscape. The frequency of this review depends on factors such as industry, market dynamics, and specific business circumstances, but as a rule of thumb, it should be considered quarterly or when significant market changes occur. Pricing strategies should carefully consider the cost structure, value to the market, supply and demand, competitive landscape, inflation, and price elasticity. Price elasticity refers to how much customers are willing to pay for your product—how flexible they are about paying more or less for what you offer. It might be time to increase your prices, which could enhance returns and business margins.

7. **Become an Investor**. The opportunity for true generational wealth lies in becoming an investor. An investor is an individual who allocates money or resources to various financial assets, ventures, or projects with the expectation of generating a return or profit. The primary goal of an investor is to grow wealth over time, either through capital appreciation, interest, dividends, or other forms of financial gain. This strategy is how Wealthy Women become the first generation of millionaires and build true generational wealth for maximum impact. Investors are masters at using money to make more money, understanding that time works in their favor.

All of these approaches can help you assess which lever to pull to increase your income generation in a joyful way. When it comes to the fundamentals, it's important to know your options for increasing income and consider which ones resonate with joyful receiving. Leveraging other people's time in a business model and system can accelerate your income faster than trading your time for money as an employee. However, even as an employee, you can still build generational wealth if you're smart. The key in every scenario is to focus on joyful receiving and creating surplus income that flows back into investments for long-term returns and asset creation. You want your money to work for you, which means that after all expenses, you have surplus funds to intentionally build wealth. In the end, you can only get to surplus in one of two ways: Make more money or reduce/hold steady your expenses as your income increases.

Whether you're an employee, self-employed, or a business owner, true wealth lies in investing for wealth creation. This leverage can change your life, change your children's lives, and help you become the first woman millionaire in your family. It will also transform your family's relationship with money for generations to come. The key to all these ideas is to lean into something new and find ways to earn more while ensuring you have a surplus to invest in building wealth. Joyfully receive, and then intentionally build. Do something that makes you a little uncomfortable, understanding that fear is just the anticipation of pain that may never come.

As women, we often forget how resilient we are. We spend time navigating certainty instead of living our best lives, knowing that we may fail but that we'll get back up. Often, the fear of failure is worse than the pain of never trying. We spend hours worrying about worst-case scenarios instead of diving into the work to build the wealthy life we desire. So go ahead and dig into joyfully creating more income for yourself.

In the next chapter, we'll explore how to command your money and make it your employee.

CONTEMPLATION QUESTIONS

Grab your Wealthy Woman notebook or use the note lines below to record your responses to these questions:

1. How would you currently describe your relationship with money?

_____

_____

_____

_____

2. Looking at your above response, does this description describe the ideal relationship you would like to have with money? Why or why not?

_____

_____

_____

_____

3. What key steps could you take today to shift your relationship in a more positive direction?

_____

_____

_____

_____

4. Do you honor your word with money? Why or why not?

_____

_____

_____

_____

5. What is your current energetic set point? Consider what is the "comfortable amount for you today."

_____

_____

_____

_____

6. What is your current income level? How can you work to increase this? What actions could you take based on where you are today?

_____

_____

_____

_____

ACTIVATIONS

1. Write a letter to your money. Write this letter as though you are in a relationship with money: Share exactly how you feel and what you would like different in the relationship.
2. Once complete, re-read the letter and see what you notice. Are there themes? Is there a recurring theme you keep playing out over and over again? What would you prefer your relationship with money to look like?

CHAPTER 7
Making Money Your Employee

Following my Spiritual Smackdown, I found myself in a devastating divorce, let go from my government job, and a single mom, as you know. Not exactly the outcome I had pinned on my vision board. Despite many nights alone, filled with regret and self-doubt, one thing I settled on for sure was that I was determined to create the best life for my son and I. I wanted a grounded place with roots, something I could call my own, to decorate as I pleased, to play soft music, and to make home-cooked meals in a happy house filled with laughter. I longed for sunshine, levity, and a space for the two of us to heal after such a tumultuous time.

After selling my marital home and paying enormous legal bills, I managed to scrape together just enough to buy a little house for us. The housing market at the time was peaking, and there were rumors of a market correction. Media stories blazed across TV and radio, broadcasting warnings of a softening market and urging people to brace for a significant reduction in home prices. I can vividly remember the well-intentioned advice I received around this time:

"Jasmine, don't buy a house."

"You're going to lose all your money."

"You don't know where you'll be in a year."

"Wait until house prices soften. It's coming."

"Renting will give you more flexibility."

"I think it's a bad decision to buy a house."

"You should ride it out and see what happens while you determine your next move."

I can still hear all this advice echoing in my ears. I listened to every word, and with loving intention, I decided to build a life for my son and me. In essence, I smiled, thanked them for their advice, and went on my merry way, ignoring it all. I followed my gut instinct without a second thought and bought a little duplex for the two of us.

It was beautiful. Three well-appointed bedrooms—one for each of us and one guest bedroom. Light streamed through the windows, and there was a little fire pit area in the backyard with a shed. It had a fully fenced pie-shaped lot where my son could play, and my little dog Molly could roam. Amid all the prior warnings and advice, I remember thinking, *This may be a terrible financial decision, but I don't care. I need to do what's right for my son and me—this is what will bring roots and joy to this moment.*

Looking back, I can't tell you how proud I am of myself. Not just for being strong enough to listen to my own Wealthy Woman intuition but also for understanding that while other people's advice was well-intentioned, it was just that—other people's advice. I was building a life for my son and me, not for them.

What I didn't realize at the time was that I was practicing what we now call head, heart, and gut thinking. Science tells us we only have one brain, which is true, but the brain is only part of our decision-making system. We actually have three decision-making centers—our head, our heart, and our gut—and they work in very different ways, but they also work together. Think about it like this:

Our head is the place of reason; our heart, the place of emotions; and our gut, the place of instinct. Our head is our rational and logical space, our analytical brain, the number-crunching expert. It weighs pros and cons, analyzes data, and adheres at all times to logic and reason. It's the voice that assesses what makes the most sense and helps us make informed decisions based on facts alone.

Our heart is the *emotion* center. Emotions aren't just passengers along for the ride; they play a critical role in our decision-making and tell us something about what we're facing. Empathy, compassion, and even fear can guide us toward choices that align (or don't) with our long-term values and goals. Our heart often asks, *What feels right?* It connects us to the human side of the equation.

Our gut is our intuition center. It's the seat of our subconscious, where past experiences, implicit knowledge, and gut feelings converge. You've likely heard it referred to as the "sixth sense" or, for women, "women's intuition." It gives us those gut warnings or nudges to take unexpected paths that sometimes make no sense on paper. We ask ourselves, *What does my gut say?* It offers valuable insights that our conscious mind can't fully comprehend.

When we get stuck with a decision, checking in with where that stuck feeling is coming from is a powerful way to enhance the decision. You can sit quietly, place your hand on your head, heart, or gut, and ask each area its perspective. It's a powerful way to determine a course of action, even within five minutes.

Learning to tune into my gut instinct and work with these three brains together has been a superpower as a Wealthy Woman. The truth is that many decisions don't make sense on paper. And if you want to be in the top 5% of Wealthy Women in the world, you must fundamentally understand that 95% of people will disagree with you, not understand where you're coming from, and certainly not validate your decision-making process. They'll offer well-intentioned advice from their perspective, which is likely not where you want to be. What I'm saying is that validation is no longer necessary. You can't seek approval or ask for advice—unless, of course, it's from someone who's already done what you want to do.

Warren Buffett famously observed this disconnect with wealth, saying, "Wall Street is the only place that people ride to in a Rolls Royce to get advice from those who take the subway." I've often thought of that. Isn't it funny? A lot of people with incredible wealth will look to others who have so much less. Why would we ever seek wealth advice from someone who has no money, no wealth, or hasn't achieved what we desire to do? As a Wealthy Woman, not only do you need to get very clear on your lifestyle alignment and be willing to put in the work, but you also need to be brave enough to take leaps that others may not understand.

This is about bringing the wealthiest version of yourself to life; understanding and fine-tuning those instincts of head, heart, and gut thinking and decision-making will serve you in your highest capacity. You must know at all times that you've got yourself covered and recognize well-meaning advice for what it is—well-intentioned—and not let it sway you, especially if the advice comes from someone who hasn't done what you aspire to do. To be in the top 5%, you need to think and act differently from the other 95%, and that takes guts. Shifting your need for external validation to internal validation is a must if you want to get there.

So, you might be wondering: What happened with that little house I bought for my family? Was it a bad decision? Should I have listened to all that advice? Well, big picture, it was the best decision I ever made. Not only because it was a beautiful home for my son and I, but also because it became my very first rental property.

When I met my now-husband, we decided to move in together and build a life. We made the brave decision to keep our individual properties and rent them out. At the time, it wasn't all roses, of course. The market did, in fact, go down. It was one of the reasons we decided to rent out our homes—I didn't want to lose money by selling mine. I was nervous, but I was ready. I loved that house for all it represented, so I was willing to take the leap of faith to rent it out instead of selling. That little house not only gave me the best years with my son as a single mom, but it also became the reason I got into real estate as an investor. Because of that small decision to buy a house, my wealth creation course was forever changed.

Sometimes, decisions are like that. We can't see the whole picture, but when we combine head, heart, and gut thinking, one decision leads to another and another. This little house allowed me to dip my toe into the world of investments and see that being a real estate investor was possible for me, too. Going against everyone's advice and making that decision was what made me believe in possibility and endless wealth creation. Yes, the market went down as everyone predicted, and I spent a few years with no appreciation, but time works for us in real estate investments. The key in real estate is simply when you buy and when you sell.

I still have that little house in my portfolio today. Not only does it generate passive income every month, but it has also appreciated over $200,000 in value. Over the last several years, when calculating the return on investment, including appreciation and cash flow, I've achieved a 640% return on my money. I'd say that's a pretty darn good return on investment (ROI)! This real estate investment has now become a security for my eldest son. Someday, I'll give it to him, or sell it, or do whatever is necessary to ensure his future is secured. Either way, if I had only made that decision using my head, ignored my heart and gut, and listened to the advice of others, I simply wouldn't be where I am today.

When it comes to intentionally creating wealth investments, there are many options. And no matter who you ask, everyone will have a different opinion. Being able to educate yourself, make decisions that align with you, and know what advice to keep and what to discard is so important to cultivating your Wealthy Woman mindset. This is not a game of comfort—it's one of growth, expansion, intuition, and move-ment. It's about holding more and making decisions that go against the grain.

Going against mainstream advice can feel contrarian because it is. But again, if you want to be in the top 5%, you'll have to think differ-ently from 95% of the population. Let me give you another practical example: When looking for investment advice, you'll often hear about diversifying your portfolio or not keeping all your eggs in one basket. The truth is that diversification is a way to avoid losing money. It's putting a little bit in various places, hoping they don't all go down. It's playing not to lose. If you want to play to win, a better strategy is to gather all the information and then select a few investments you truly believe will grow. That's how you make money.

Now that you know you're in a relationship with money, you must trust, take risks, and build assets in the form of investments. You need to make money your employee and activate your head, heart, and gut thinking. Like with income generation, the idea with investments is to get your money working for you in a way that brings you joy, challenges you, excites you, and makes you passionate about learning. You've got to fall in love with the idea of creating joyful wealth freedom. You also need the time, patience, and tenacity to decide you want it and to stay the course. Wealthy Women understand the long game, and you're in it for the long haul.

Making money your employee means that you are no longer trading time for money. Rather, the investments you are creating are building wealth for you while you sleep. It's a strategy of investing and managing your finances in such a way that money works for you rather than you working solely for money. The concept here is about leveraging financial resources to generate more wealth or income, much like a productive employee contributes to a business's success. Here are some ways that you can get your money working for you:

1. **The Stock Market.** The stock market is a collection of exchanges and markets where securities, such as stocks, bonds, and other financial instruments, are bought and sold. It provides a platform for companies to raise capital by issuing shares of stock to investors, and it offers investors the opportunity to buy and sell ownership in these companies. Investing in individual stocks or exchange-traded funds (ETFs) can yield significant returns. The stock market offers opportunities for compound growth, dividend payments, long-term appreciation, and even tax advantages.

2. **Real Estate Investments.** This one, as you may have already pieced together, is my favorite. Andrew Carnegie once said that 90% of all millionaires become so through owning real estate. That's staggering, but it makes complete sense to me. Real estate investing offers so much, including the opportunity for passive cash flow, appreciation, federal tax benefits, leverage, refinance options, and the ability to improve housing and communities. If you don't want to be a landlord or hire a property manager, you can also invest in real estate investment trusts (REITs). They are a great way to invest in real estate without having to directly own property.

3. **Mutual Funds.** These are professionally managed investment funds that pool money from many investors to purchase securities.

4. **Cryptocurrency.** Digital currencies like Bitcoin and Ethereum have shown potential for high returns, though they come with high risk and volatility.

5. **Peer-to-Peer Lending.** These platforms facilitate loans between individuals, providing high returns, though they come with a higher risk compared to traditional investments.

6. **Retirement Accounts.** Contributing to retirement accounts like 401(k)s or IRAs (or RRSPs for my Canadian friends) offers tax advantages and long-term potential growth. Many employers offer matching contributions, enhancing growth. One thing to consider here is to always be aware of how much you're paying in fees for these accounts to be managed on your behalf.

7. **Alternative Investments.** This category includes private equity, hedge funds, collectibles, or venture capital. These investments can offer incredibly high returns but are often less liquid, require higher initial investments, and may have unpredictable timelines.

As you consider which of these strategies will best help make your money your employee, you'll also need to consider your risk tolerance. Understand your appetite for risk and your ability to handle discomfort, and invest accordingly. That brings me to the next factor: the time horizon. Consider how long you plan to hold an investment before needing access to the funds. Next, educate yourself on key areas of interest for investment.

Stay informed about market trends and continuously educate yourself about shifts in your chosen investment vertical. For example, in real estate, you should always be aware of interest rates, lending prices, market demand, and rental legislation. These are key items I constantly scan for, adjusting our portfolio as needed. If you're new to investing, you may want to consider a mentor, coach, or professional advice. You can consult with a financial advisor to help tailor your investment strategy to your financial goals.

However, be mindful of fees and costs associated with these services, as high fees can significantly erode your wealth over time. Seeking advice and making your own informed decisions is different from outsourcing responsibility for your money. Get involved, learn the game, and be ready to ask questions when seeking advice from a financial advisor.

Over time, I've refined my preferred investment strategy to focus on real estate. I love improving communities and housing for renters and being the best landlord around, and I honestly love the thrill of finding a deal. Of course, I have other things in my portfolio, including traditional investments, cryptocurrency, and private equity. But my favorite method for making money work for me is through real estate.

It's interesting to me that if you google "Should I invest in real estate or traditional investments," you'll inevitably find an article comparing the average real estate equity appreciation of 3% to stock market returns of 7%. One thing to note is that these articles often reflect the author's or reader's beliefs. It's funny how humans always build stories to align with their beliefs—welcome to confirmation bias. Confirmation bias is the tendency to seek out, interpret, or remember information in a way that confirms one's preexisting beliefs or opinions. This can lead to skewed perceptions and reinforce existing viewpoints, even when there's contradictory evidence. Being aware of your confirmation bias can help you interpret new data objectively. As a Wealthy Woman, you need to take in new information without judgment and make your own decisions, including when I share my story and why I believe real estate is such an amazing wealth generator. Also, always consider if the advice is coming from someone who has DONE what you desire to do - this makes a world of difference.

One of the reasons I love real estate as a wealth generator is because it's a trifecta of leverage. Let me give you an example. I bring in joyful income through the value I generate in the world, and I receive it with grace. Then, rather than depositing it into my savings account, I start thinking about how I can leverage it and get it working for me. Let's use a little house that I purchased as a single mom as an example. I had managed to scrape together $30,000. I took that $30,000 to the bank and got a mortgage to access $300,000. Let's say $300,000, for simplicity's sake. I then used that mortgage to purchase a home, locking in the price. Then, I rented it out to a tenant who pays my monthly mortgage. In fact, not only does it generate a little extra cash flow each month, but I also benefit as the tenant pays off the mortgage while the house appreciates in value. This is the trifecta of leverage. I leverage my money with the bank to get more, I set the price of an appreciating asset, and I have someone else pay off the loan for me. It's leverage on leverage on leverage.

You might be wondering, what about property management and maintenance? No question, owning real estate is work. But if this little house brings in the average 3% annual appreciation, I'm not only earning that appreciation but also getting the leverage from the bank, cash flow from the house, and having someone else pay off the debt in my name. And I can leverage this even further. I can access the $200,000 in equity that the house has appreciated by refinancing if I choose. If I do that, I can take that cash and buy another house or two, replicating the success. Rinse and repeat. You can see how this approach can gain momentum, and before you know it, I'm making money in my sleep—officially, money becomes my employee. And for those who fear dealing with maintenance issues or late-night texts, don't worry—there are property management companies for that.

The worst advice I've ever received—well-intentioned, of course—is to pay off my mortgage. While that might make me feel comfortable, at the end of the day, I'd be sitting on a bunch of dead money. Dead money refers to funds that aren't working for you but are sitting stagnant and not earning more. It's like having a squatter in your financial life. If you're willing to expand your thinking and trust yourself more, you might realize you have a lot of money that could create massive wealth for you but is just sitting there, stagnant, under the guise of doing the "right thing" or as dead money in your savings account.

If you are committed to making money your employee, you'll also want to invest time and energy into understanding estate planning. Estate planning involves organizing and managing your assets to ensure efficient transfer to heirs and beneficiaries after your death. It includes creating wills, trusts, and other legal arrangements to minimize estate taxes and avoid probate. Effective estate planning preserves wealth across generations and ensures that your assets are distributed according to your wishes. Think of it as an insurance policy for your wealth. No one wants to leave a giant tax bill to their loved ones and see their wealth disappear.

The freedom and calm that making money my employee has brought into my life is immeasurable. When I was working a job, I used to imagine that the job was secure. I grew up with the idea that getting a good job with a retirement pension would secure my future. But through my experience, I learned that security doesn't really exist —it's just a false construct. While that might feel uncomfortable, embracing the idea that nothing is truly secure brings great freedom. Building multiple streams of income on my own terms has been my true freedom. To know that I can wake up and do what I want without the pressure of necessity is immense. It has allowed me to bloom into the most free, joyful, creative, and wealthy version of myself. It has given me steady cash flow and the ultimate financial freedom of choice for my time. It's been a magic wand, creating a life of financial happiness, joy, and freedom.

Investments can include creating businesses, traditional investing, or real estate, but whatever you choose, have fun with it. In the end, it's about focus, intention, commitment to the long-term vision, and living your best life. Intentional wealth generation through investment, value, and asset creation is key.

As more money has flowed into my life through joyful receiving, ironically, it has become less and less about money for me and more about how I can bring value to the world and shift generational money beliefs in my family. It's about how I can use my voice and experience to lift other women to their wealthiest, happiest selves. I deeply believe that money in the hands of conscious women is good for the world. This approach has allowed me to build a long-term, sustainable legacy for my children, to consciously shift the paradigm for my three little boys so they can live their heart's desires, bring their best value to the world, and make their dreams a reality. As a mother and matriarch of my family, nothing brings me more joy than seeing their eyes light up with possibility, knowing they can make it a reality. Doing this for not only my family but for thousands of women across the globe is now my mission.

In the next chapter, we'll explore activation and movement. While reading this book has been vital for illuminating ideas, you'll only shift your life to its wealthiest version through action and movement. The ability to hold discomfort as you take brave steps forward will ulti-mately shift the foundation of your life and fill your bank account to the brim.

REFLECTION QUESTIONS

Alright, you get it! Grab the Wealthy Woman notebook or use the note lines below and let's get contemplating. Here are the reflection ques-tions for this chapter:

1. How do I typically make decisions? Do I favor my head, heart, or gut? Or do I use all three centers actively? Has my approach served me well? Why or why not?

_____

_____

_____

_____

2. When making decisions, do I often consult others for their opinion? If so, is this for information purposes or validation of my idea?

_____

_____

_____

_____

3. Who do I most seek validation from in my decision-making? How would it feel if I did not receive that validation?

_____

_____

_____

_____

4. What can I do to fine-tune my own knowledge and trust I don't need external validation?

_____

_____

_____

_____

5. How can I make money my "employee" and get it working harder for me? What is a key step I could take to bring this to life?

_____

_____

_____

_____

6. Do I have dead money in my portfolio that could be working harder for me? How can I get it working harder for me?

_____

_____

_____

_____

7. Do I have an estate plan? Why or why not?

_____

_____

_____

_____

ACTIVATIONS

1. If you have investments (this can be retirement savings, education savings, regular savings, etc.), determine how much your return on investment has been in this last year (this will be a percentage).
2. If you have investments with a financial advisor, determine how much you pay in fees each year. Now subtract that from your annual return to confirm the amount you actually made on a percentage basis.
3. If you don't have one already, engage someone to assist you in building an estate plan and will. This is key to ensuring you protect your assets, wealth, and loved ones.

CHAPTER 8

Expansion and Bravery

"Being Brave is not being unafraid, but feeling the fear and doing it anyway... when you feel the fear, try using it as a signal that something really important is about to happen."
–Gloria Steinem

During my MBA program, I took a class called Entrepreneurship. One of the assignments was networking. Oh, the dread of networking! I think walking into a room full of strangers to network was the thing I feared most at that point in my life. I don't know what it is about networking that gets everyone tied in knots—maybe it's the lack of confidence, the pressure to say something interesting, or perhaps I was just too shy or self-conscious to break the ice. But honestly, I felt like I was going to vomit when I saw that it was our next assignment. At that moment, it felt like the worst thing in the world looming before me.

As a rule, back then, I preferred to fade into the background, never to be seen or take up space. In hindsight, I can't really blame myself. As women, we're often told by society and the media to look pretty, not take up too much space, and remain agreeable. Nonetheless, this was definitely an exercise in expansion for me, and I could feel it in every part of my body. I was nervous. My palms were sweaty, and I even lost sleep over it. There was a moment where I considered just not doing it. I didn't need this silly exercise anyway. I'm sure you can relate to this in your life. But one of my core beliefs was that I was a "good girl" who followed the rules, so there was no way I wasn't going to do the assignment.

My mission was to obtain ten business cards from others at the event. So, I bit the bullet, signed up for a local networking event for students, and off I went, awkwardly armed with my newly minted business cards for trade. Walking into that room, it felt like everyone was already talking in groups or busy doing their own thing. I could feel the nerves rising up inside me. It seemed like no matter where I looked, I was intruding on a conversation. Then, finally, I spotted an opportunity. With sweaty palms, I marched over to a young woman standing alone, looking just as awkward as I did. Perfect. This was my chance to get my first business card. I approached her with my sweaty hands extended and said:

"Hi, I'm Jasmine. What's your name?"

To my surprise, I saw a wave of relief wash over her face. Maybe she had a silly assignment, too. Then something amazing happened. I just kept asking her questions with genuine curiosity. It turned out she loved music and hated networking events, too. We connected instantly. I learned all sorts of interesting things about her, including that she knew someone who could help me with an upcoming project. And I didn't have to say a single thing about myself. In that instant, I realized networking wasn't about me at all. I could drop the pressure of trying to say something impressive. I didn't have to worry about what I had to offer. It was about simple human connection, genuine curiosity, and just learning about others.

I thought, *What if networking was about making others feel comfortable? What if I decided it was my mission to ease the awkwardness others felt, just as I did? To spend time learning about others and making them feel better?* Maybe, if I was lucky, I'd make a valuable connection. What if I didn't have to worry about impressing anyone at all? What if all I needed to do was take the first step and be genuinely interested in other people?

Looking back, this little networking assignment changed my life and perspective forever. Networking didn't need to be about me shining in a room or one-upping anyone, which is what always made me feel uncomfortable. Instead, what if I didn't have to share anything about myself at all? What if all I had to do was ask questions of the other person? Not only would I build richer, more meaningful connections, but it also took away all the pressure of needing to say something interesting. That's not to say I won't answer if someone asks. The person who asks me, "What's the most exciting thing you're learning right now?" might just hit the jackpot. But I urge you to try this approach the next time you're at a networking event. Expand in a way that's altruistic in nature. Focus on those around you, be genuinely curious, and connect with people. You might be surprised by how much people enjoy being around you when you take a genuine interest in who they are as individuals.

As a truly wealthy, abundant woman, one of the most important skills is the ability to be brave and expand into new spaces. As you shift into your highest abundance and wealth, there will be moments that stretch you beyond where you are today. And our human bodies, both fortunately and unfortunately, are hardwired to keep us in our comfort zones. This can be great if you're already where you want to be, but if you desire more, you'll need to be intentional about reaching for those new, wealth-abundant heights.

As you strive for more, you'll activate your nervous system. You'll feel those sweaty palms, butterflies, and nervousness that I experienced at that networking event. Your body will do everything it can to keep you where you are. In my example, not only did I have a pit in my stomach and feel nauseous, but there were physical symptoms that came with stepping into something I hadn't done before. This is often the first signal that you are expanding. One issue I've noticed with clients is that they sometimes interpret these nervous feelings as a sign that they shouldn't be doing something instead of recognizing it as a normal response to growth. Sometimes, we confuse our body's normal reactions with the idea that we're on the wrong path when, in fact, we're just expanding into something new. This can cause us to shrink back into old routines.

Most of the clients I work with are complete bosses who have built all they have through their own fortitude, not necessarily coming from money. They didn't grow up with a silver spoon and often come from households with a comfort mindset. Growing up, they were not well-off—at best, middle class. But through hard work and perseverance, they've accomplished amazing things in their lives: top executive jobs, CEO positions, business ownership, and entrepreneurship. However, despite their success, they haven't been taught how to build true wealth.

As we dive into doing more—buying real estate, launching companies, and expanding to create more wealth—we, as women who are joyful first-generation millionaires, need to understand how our nervous systems can either help or hinder us as we expand and become more intentional.

Because, at the end of the day, leaning in is not enough. We must be brave. We must expand on purpose and get into rooms with people from whom we can learn. You may need to face those sweaty palms, butterflies, and that nervousness, hold yourself steady, and do it anyway. You've likely heard the saying, "If you're the smartest person in the room, you're in the wrong room." This is exactly what this refers to: You need to build genuine connections and activate intentional expansion by getting into close proximity with people who have already done what you desire to do. Your network is your net worth, and connection is key. Expansion through connection is a necessary ingredient for success.

NERVOUS SYSTEM ACTIVATION

Doing something new, trying on new wealthy ideas, and taking risks will often activate your nervous system. It's important to understand how it works, so you can not only be aware of it but also learn how to regulate it, allowing you to expand despite those feelings.

The nervous system is a complex, highly organized network that enables communication between different parts of your body and coordinates its functions. It's composed of the central nervous system (the brain and spinal cord) and the peripheral nervous system, which connects the central nervous system to the rest of the body. Your brain acts as the control center, processing sensory information, generating thoughts and emotions, and initiating responses. The spinal cord transmits signals between the brain and your peripheral nerves. Within the peripheral nervous system, the somatic nervous system controls voluntary movements and transmits sensory information, while the autonomic nervous system regulates involuntary functions such as heart rate, digestion, and respiratory rate—think sweaty palms at a networking event or the pit in your stomach before a big meeting.

The autonomic nervous system is further divided into two areas: the sympathetic nervous system, which prepares your body for fight-or-flight responses during stress, and the parasympathetic nervous system, which promotes rest and digestion during calm periods. These two centers were vital for survival when humans were cave dwellers. If there were a saber-tooth tiger nearby, the sympathetic nervous system would kick into high gear to protect us.

In a well-regulated system, the body can quickly shift from a fight-or-flight response back into the parasympathetic system of *rest* and *digest*. Over time, staying in a heightened state can lead to chronic fatigue, burnout, and anxiety. Nowadays, we don't face threats like saber-tooth tigers, but our nervous system is still scanning for danger. When you activate a new idea or attempt to expand your wealth, your system may flip on and perceive the unknown as a threat. Next thing you know, you're activating your *fight, flight,* or *freeze* response.

It's imperative to recognize that just because you're feeling that way, it doesn't necessarily mean you shouldn't proceed. Understanding the difference between your autonomic nervous system's response and simply avoiding something new is crucial. Being aware of your nervous system's activation is important as you expand your wealth, take risks, and accept more responsibility. The pursuit of growth often involves increased stress and pressure, which can strain the nervous system. By managing and regulating your nervous system, you can better assess whether something is truly a threat or simply your body's auto-response to the unknown.

Regulating your nervous system also improves mental and physical health, both essential for sustaining high levels of productivity and performance as you seek to expand wealth and abundance. A well-regulated nervous system supports cognitive functions like focus, memory, and decision-making, all of which are crucial to navigating new ideas, wealth expansions, and challenges. It also enhances emotional resilience, allowing you to handle setbacks and stressors with composure and effectiveness as you expand and take brave steps forward.

There are some key strategies I've used over the years, both personally and with clients, to help regulate your nervous system.

For a moment, imagine you're dropping into wealth creation and exploring new ways to get your money working for you. Let's say, for example, you want to purchase your first piece of real estate. You might get butterflies and sweaty palms. It's a new challenge—you've never done this before, and your system is fully activated. But you know, deep down, this is something you truly want to do. Here are some great tips that you can use to really move through and hold yourself as your nervous system activates:

1. **Activate your higher consciousness.** In moments when you feel truly dysregulated but know deep in your soul that you want to move forward, you can hand your worries over to your higher consciousness. By this, I mean to hand the reins over to your spirit, higher power, God, the universe— whatever resonates with you. Money and material things, after all, are just the output of an inner world of riches and beliefs. Trusting the universe and acknowledging a higher power working to your advantage can be incredibly regulating. You can literally say aloud or in prayer: "Universe, I need some assistance here—please guide me to the outcome for my highest good. I am handing my worries

over to you and would like you to ensure it all works out for me."

2. **Ground yourself.** Put your feet on the grass and ground yourself. Sometimes, when I'm taking a big risk, I will take off my shoes and socks and place my bare feet on the ground. Close your eyes and imagine roots shooting out of the bottom of your feet, connecting you to the earth. In these moments, repeat a mantra like, "I am safe, whole, and capable, and no matter what happens, this will work out."

3. **Practice deep breathing exercises.** Engage in diaphragm breathing to activate the parasympathetic nervous system, promoting relaxation and reducing stress. You can try exercises like "ha" breathing, where you take short, quick breaths followed by a big exhale. I'll often tell my little five-year-old, "Smell a flower, blow a candle," and it works.

4. **Mindfulness, meditation, and visualization.** Spend a few minutes each day practicing mindfulness to stay present, reduce stress, and improve regulation. Visualize the best-case scenario, feel the joy in your body when it works out, and act today as if it will go your way. Picture it in your mind's eye, say affirmations, and manifest it into reality.

5. **Get moving.** Physical activities like yoga, weight lifting, walking, or dancing release endorphins, which are natural stress relievers. These help regulate your nervous system and bring it back down to a calm state.

6. **Eat nourishing food.** When stressed or overwhelmed, it's easy to slip into poor eating habits. Be mindful of maintaining a balanced diet that is rich in fruits, vegetables, lean proteins, and whole grains. This will support your body and brain function, keeping you in top form as you make important decisions.

7. **Hydrate.** Drink plenty of water throughout the day to keep your body functioning optimally. Dehydration can exacerbate stress and cognitive decline, so staying hydrated is essential to prevent further nervous system dysregulation.

8. **Connect with loved ones.** Spending time with family and friends or sharing a snuggle with my son or husband helps build a strong support network. This reduces feelings of isolation and mitigates stress. It's amazing how far a simple hug from someone you love can go. Remind yourself that you already have what you need to be wealthy, happy, and joyful, regardless of whether your current endeavor succeeds or fails.

9. **Catch some shut-eye.** Ensure you get enough quality sleep each night to support your overall health and stress management. Sleep is vital for restoring energy, improving cognitive function, regulating emotions, balancing hormones, and facilitating recovery. While it's easy to lose sleep during stressful times, establishing a good sleep routine is essential for rejuvenation. Aim for seven to nine hours of sleep per night.

Acknowledging when your body feels nervous and engaging in some of the activities mentioned above can help your body drop out of dysregulation and activate the parasympathetic nervous system, also known as the "rest and digest" system. While the fight-or-flight system is important, the key is not to stay in that state too long. If your body remains there for an extended period, you risk burnout, anxiety, and chronic stress—the opposite of what you want to achieve. We are aiming for joy, happiness, and freedom—a joyful first-generation millionaire. The key here is to acknowledge that as you shift and seek higher wealth consciousness, translating these into material changes in your world, it will feel uncomfortable. That discomfort is just your human nervous system doing its job. Being aware of its activations and having tools to manage that discomfort will help you stand firm, take action, and recognize that nervousness is a natural bodily response—not a sign that you shouldn't move forward.

Quite frankly, you will likely experience this discomfort repeatedly as you expand. Getting good at facing fear, regulating or holding discomfort, and taking action despite your nerves will unlock your next level of wealth and abundance. At times, it will be easy to freeze, flee, or fawn into inaction. But none of these options will lead to the wealth and abundance you desire. Similar to that networking event, you must make the decision to act and commit. Honor your word to yourself and do what needs to be done, even with sweaty palms. I'm not suggesting you make decisions without thought or consideration, but if you know there's something you deeply desire in your soul's wisdom, sometimes the only way through is to feel the fear and do it anyway. By holding yourself through nervous system dysregulation and taking action, you will actually build new neural pathways for that activity. Next time, your nervous system won't be as activated. Your body will recognize that there is no saber-tooth tiger ahead—just another notch on your experience belt.

Much has been taught about women "leaning in," and for this, I am eternally grateful, but I wish to enrich the conversation by noting that being at the table is less important than being in the right room. There was a time when I couldn't afford to be in the VIP section or even at the table, but just being in the room was enough to start absorbing information. Being in close proximity to those who have done what you want to do allows you not only to absorb their knowledge, thinking, and energy but also inspires you to move toward your desires. Practicing being in the right rooms is critical for any woman aspiring to become the first joyful millionaire in her family.

These "right rooms" are spaces where influential conversations happen, decisions are made, and opportunities are presented. By positioning yourself in such environments, you can access valuable networks, gain insights from those who have already achieved significant success, and potentially secure mentorship from individuals who can offer guidance and support. Learning from those who have already done what you aspire to do is essential in a game where you aim to differentiate yourself from the average. Being in these rooms also means staying informed about industry trends, potential investments, and strategic partnerships. It's about being visible and vocal in the circles that matter, which can open doors to opportunities that would otherwise remain out of reach. So certainly, if you're at the table, lean in. But if you're not there yet, focus on getting in the room. Be in the room, buy the ticket, attend the professional development, hire the coach—do whatever it takes to be in close proximity to those who have done what you want to do.

Exercising bravery is equally important on this journey. Bravery involves stepping out of your comfort zone, taking calculated risks, and facing your fears head-on. For a woman aiming to break financial barriers and create a legacy of wealth and joy, bravery requires resilience in the face of setbacks and the ability to persevere through challenges. Bravery is also about self-advocacy, demanding fair treatment, negotiating better deals, and asserting your value in professional settings. This courageous, confident mindset helps you overcome societal and internalized barriers that often hold women back from achieving their full potential.

The combination of being in the right room and exercising bravery lays a strong foundation for becoming a joyful first-generation millionaire. By actively seeking influential environments and demonstrating courage in your actions, you can set a powerful example not just for yourself but also for future generations. You'll not only build your own wealth but also pave the way for a legacy of empowerment and possibility for women across the world. This journey is about more than just financial success—it's about creating and cultivating joy, fulfillment, and a sense of purpose. It's about breaking the cycle of financial struggle that has perpetuated within your family for generations and creating a brighter, more prosperous future for yourself, your family, and your community. It's about cultivating connection and being the woman who says, "I know an amazing woman who can help with that!"

In the next chapter, we'll explore the importance of putting our knowledge into action so that your wealth reality begins to unfold right before your eyes.

REFLECTION QUESTIONS

Grab your sacred notebook or use the note lines below, as we are getting deep to the core! Here are the contemplation questions for this chapter:

1. When did I last experience my nervous system being activated?

_____

_____

_____

_____

2. How did I know my nervous system was activated?

_____

_____

_____

_____

3. Did I try to regulate myself? If so, how?

_____

_____

_____

_____

4. Did I leap in fear or shrink back after I felt all the nerves? Why or why not?

_____

_____

_____

_____

5. How do I feel about networking and getting into new rooms? Why do I feel this way?

_____

_____

_____

_____

6. How does reframing being curious about others take the pressure off my need to shine? Do I notice myself trying to shine, or do I allow others to speak? Why or why not?

_____

_____

_____

_____

ACTIVATIONS

1. Find a room, group, or meet-up with people who are doing something you deeply desire to learn about or understand. Join the group and introduce yourself; share your desires—specifically, and that you are there to learn.
2. Attend a networking group and activate your curiosity.
3. Determine which key regulation tactics you will use next time your nervous system gets activated to try and ground yourself.

CHAPTER 9
Action Over Perfection

"The most difficult decision is the decision to act, the rest is merely tenacity.
The fears are paper tigers. You can do anything you decide to do.
You can act to change and control your life and
the procedure, the process is its own reward."
–Amelia Earhart

While I was on maternity leave with my third son, I had a lot of time to contemplate what we wanted to do next. I'm grateful that in Canada, the government affords 12 months off to new mothers. And while there was a dip in our income, it was enough to get by for a year, allowing me to spend much-needed bonding time with my new arrival. As I nursed my small son, a seed of an idea was born: What if we could bring in more cash flow through real estate while improving access to affordable housing for potential renters?

With the birth of my children, my previous vision of a career-driven woman at the top no longer fit my desires. Long hours commuting and seeing my children so little wasn't where my heart was anymore. It was time for a shift, and as scary as it was, I had to dive into these new desires. I realized that more than anything, I wanted freedom of time to spend with my children, nurture their lives, and have more adventures with my family. I wanted to be present. If something went wrong, I wanted to be the first to know and to be there by their side as they learned how to pivot for their highest good. I wanted to make sure I was truly present for the gift of being their mother. I didn't want anyone but me raising.

As a side note, I know many mothers choose to have help and nannies, and I think that's amazing. For me, being personally present was my desire, but I celebrate every woman for choosing the path that feels aligned with her journey as a mother. I started to imagine a world where we created assets that paid us each month while becoming the best landlords the world had ever seen. We had been saving for some time and had enough money to purchase not one but two more properties for our portfolio.

Now, I want to pause here and acknowledge that this may feel out of reach for many, but I assure you that when you put your mind to something and focus on it, one small step at a time, you, too, can save a down payment for your first property. Decision, belief, tenacity, and discipline can get you anywhere you desire. There was only one problem: COVID had just ended. Interest rates were on the rise, competition was insane, and it was a hot, hot, hot seller's market. Most real estate investors would tell you to sell in a seller's market and buy in a buyer's market. We were doing the literal opposite. Yet, my head, heart, and gut told me to go for it, even though it didn't make sense logically or on paper. Houses were receiving multiple offers, and many people advised against purchasing real estate because I would pay too much. But I had learned with our previous two homes that the only thing that really matters is when you buy and when you sell, and in the end, time would work in our favor. My deep intuition told me that the time was now.

My husband was on board, and off we went to get pre-approved for a couple of mortgages with our little boy in tow. The first house we found was in a suburban community. We already had two properties there, and I had become a bit of an expert in knowing which types of properties were in demand and would rent quickly. I viewed hundreds of houses and vetted property after property, running Excel spreadsheets to ensure they would cash flow until the right one came up. Finally, the perfect one hit the market.

It was in immaculate condition, located in a wonderful family community, with three bedrooms, two baths, and a small backyard. The numbers made sense. I could rent it for a reasonable amount to a great tenant, with all expenses completely covered and a small profit each month after accounting for maintenance and other needs. Miraculously, it had no offers. So, with a swift bid, I was able to lock it in at $15,000 under the list price—an incredible feat in a seller's market. Even my realtor couldn't believe it. I was thrilled. On to the next one.

The market continued heating up, with rates climbing and bidding wars getting more intense. Bid after bid, I lost house after house. It was so competitive, and I was getting frustrated, searching day and night to find the right property.

My realtor had set up notifications, so I would be pinged immediately when anything new came on the market. Finally, a house I had previously had my eye on came back on the market—the buyer's financing had fallen through, and the sellers were looking to secure a solid offer quickly. I knew exactly what to do. I bid on it, sight unseen. I was terrified, literally in a full state of nervous system dysregulation, but we placed a full-price offer 20 minutes after it came back on the market. I hadn't even seen it. Despite the fear, I knew it was the right move, and 24 hours later, the house was ours.

There had been seven more bids after ours within 24 hours, but the sellers felt reassured that our financing position was solid, so they picked our offer—they didn't want another deal to fall through. However, they added an unusual condition: We had to come and see the house before finalizing the paperwork. No problem. I loaded my tiny son into his car seat, and off we went to see our potential new rental property. As I drove, music playing in the background, I thought to myself, *I'm so proud. We did it.* We finally pulled up to that quaint little house with its turquoise blue front.

From the outside, it was picture-perfect. I loaded my son into my front carrier, and our realtor greeted us. We unlocked the front door, and as I stepped inside, I instantly felt sick to my stomach. Oh no. What had we done? It turns out that one thing you can't see in an online listing is the smell. I guess there's no "scratch and sniff" feature for real estate listings. The smell was overwhelming—feral cats gone wild. The stench of cat pee was everywhere I turned. It was truly outrageous, something that made my stomach turn instantly. And it wasn't just the smell. There were doors off their hinges, DIY lace on the windows, and slapdash renovations. The pictures hadn't captured the disarray, and I was standing there, jaw dropped, in person.

I quickly estimated that there was at least $10,000 worth of damage that needed to be fixed. No wonder they wanted us to come and see it. A wave of dread rippled through my body and settled in my stomach —enter full-on nervous system dysregulation. By most people's definition, this was a money pit.

Upon inspection, we discovered a leak behind the bathtub, destroying the drywall behind the shower. It needed to be replaced due to water damage and potential mold—yet another expense. I could feel my palms getting damp. That night, I felt sick to my stomach. Was this a warning sign that I shouldn't go through with it, or should I stay the course? I took a shower, practiced some deep breathing and visualization, and tucked in to get some shut-eye.

After a restless sleep, we went back to the seller and asked for money to cover the repairs. We knew that most of the damage, while off-putting, was cosmetic. It was a risk, with seven other offers waiting in the wings. The sellers were agreeable and gave us $12,000 off the purchase price. Throughout the deal, I practiced my nervous system regulators regularly. I walked, meditated, handed my worries over to my higher consciousness, and did yoga every morning. I reminded myself that we were safe whether this worked out or not. But if we moved forward, we'd have one more great rental in our portfolio and a lovely home for a tenant once the repairs were complete.

Our realtor helped us find a wonderful handyman contractor, and within two weeks, all the repairs were completed. The home was rented to a lovely couple who had just moved across the country. Both of these little homes are still in our portfolio today.

As we wind through this journey of wealth and abundance together, one thing I want you to understand more than anything is that there will always be a reason not to do something. Whether people disagree, the timing doesn't feel right, the numbers aren't perfect, or maybe it's just fear. But the real truth is, it's not the things you don't do that change your life—it's the things you move on, the things you do, the actions you take. Literally, the "no's" in your life don't matter. They change nothing. The doors that close and the opportunities that never come to fruition have zero impact on your life. What changes your life are the actions you take—the yeses you say yes to, the doors that open because of your choices.

What I really want to emphasize is that there is no perfect buy, perfect move, perfect reel, perfect time, or perfect strategy. It's all about energetically aligning your beliefs with emotions and embodying who you want to become, which means taking aligned, massive action in the direction of your desires. It's action over perfection that will change your life every single time.

When you seek to take action and do something you've never done before, your sympathetic nervous system will flip you into fight-or-flight mode, and there are common responses that can occur beyond what we've already discussed. You might find yourself engaging in controlling behavior, trying to ensure the outcome is perfect, or asserting dominance to reduce the chance of failure. This could show up as urgency to solve an issue or sending multiple emails or communications to get someone to do something to ease the pressure. When we do this, we cut off the infinite possibilities from the divine, often leading to burnout or fatigue.

You might also start overthinking. When overwhelmed, some people become paralyzed and unable to make decisions, leading to missed opportunities and stagnation. Overthinking is a common freeze response, where you get trapped in a cycle of analysis and worry, unable to move forward. The problem with overthinking and doing nothing is that doing nothing is a decision—a decision to stay exactly where you are. You might also bury your head in the sand to avoid the trigger or dive deep into distractions. This can be a flight response, where someone immerses themselves in work or mindless activities, like Netflix, to avoid making decisions or taking action. This is procrastination.

Another response could be people-pleasing. You might find yourself doing things to please others rather than listening to your own spiritual guidance or seeking validation from others that you're doing the right thing. This might manifest as excessive agreeableness, where you prioritize others' needs over your own to avoid conflict or gain approval. It can also show up as difficulty setting boundaries or constantly seeking reassurance. The challenge with people-pleasing is that if you want to be among the top wealth earners, validation from others can't be your compass. People-pleasing and seeking validation will definitely lead you off course. Over the years, I've learned that it's taking action that allows me to expand the most.

But here's the good news: Something beautiful awaits you on the other side of action. Once you move forward and take action, your body realizes that it is, in fact, safe. Those activities and things that once felt so expansive become easier to reach. Your body starts to categorize them as safe, and you won't be as activated the next time you take the same leap. You begin to understand that it's not as scary, dangerous, or fearsome as you once anticipated. I've learned that the worst-case scenario is always far worse in our minds than it ever turns out to be. Time and time again, I've shown myself that despite the fear, I'm safe to leap and try something new. We're human, and our nervous system will activate, but that's not a sign to stop—it's a sign to pause, breathe, and acknowledge that this is your body's natural response to doing something unfamiliar. The other side is always far less intimidating than your imagination would have you believe. Often, the fear that paralyzes us is harder to bear than just taking action and discovering what's on the other side.

Today, when I buy a new house, commercial property, or multiunits as a real estate investor, I don't get sweaty palms or a pit in my stomach. Even if something doesn't look perfect on paper or smells like cat pee, I've got that experience under my belt now. When my nervous system activates, I can regulate it. It was holding the discomfort and taking action anyway that got me to the other side of that fear —and it will do the same for you!

Action breaks the cycle of procrastination and builds confidence through small, achievable steps. It fosters progress and growth, helping you overcome fear and self-doubt. By taking action, you create opportunities, learn from experience, and move closer to your goals. Without action, even the best ideas and intentions remain unrealized, leading to frustration and stagnation. Consistent action builds discipline and resilience—essential qualities for long-term success and fulfillment.

Taking action is like a muscle we can strengthen. The more you exercise your action-oriented muscle, the easier it gets. At first, it requires a lot of energy and focus, but with practice, it becomes second nature. You honor your word so deeply to yourself that it becomes automatic to follow through on your commitments.

Sometimes, when we have an idea, we think, *Okay, I need to set aside time for that.* But then, the sun is shining, something else pressing pops up, and it never happens. But if you break your big goals down into small, manageable parts or put yourself in a position where you have to take action (like the six steps above), everything shifts. Let me tell you about a time I decided to write a book. Did you know that I had this book in my heart for almost seven years? That's a long time to hold a universal, divine idea inside. The day I finally sprang into action, I realized that if I could help just one woman transform her life from unhappiness to financial freedom, abundance, and her wealthiest self, it would be worth writing.

If this book has helped you in any way, please feel free to connect with me on social media—I'd love to hear from you. As soon as my goal of writing the book became about helping others rather than just getting my idea out there, everything shifted quickly. I purchased a writing course, and then a publisher who helps writers get published reached out to me on Instagram. The rest is history. And here I am, finally writing my book to share the wisdom of wealth I've curated in my life. I had to take massive, embodied action, and then the universe responded.

Another way to shift into action is to simply try it on. This might be my favorite thing. Imagine who you desire to be in great detail. Where does she hang out? What does she drive? What does she like to eat? Who is she? Get as specific as possible, and then go be that person. If you desire to have a spa day in the middle of the week—*go do it*. If you want to be a real estate investor, introduce yourself as such. If you desire to have beautiful clothes, be thoughtful about what you wear. Want to reignite the romance in your relationship? Slip on your sexiest clothes and make it happen. You can apply this approach to any area of your life. Just go try it on.

Sometimes, thinking about the bigger picture feels overwhelming, but breaking it down into smaller parts helps. Instead of worrying about how it will all come together, focus on one small action at a time. Create an intentional to-do list with mini-steps along the way—a sort of reverse engineering. There were moments in my real estate investing career and coaching business when I didn't know how it was going to work. But instead of taking on the entire responsibility at once, I broke it down into tiny, manageable steps, tackling one thing at a time. Don't worry about the big picture—just focus on one small piece at a time. Here are some steps you can take to reverse engineer your wealth goal and snap it into action:

1. **Clearly define your goal** as it relates to wealth, abundance, and freedom. Be as specific as possible—generalizations won't work. For example, "I want to make $50,000 of passive income through real estate."
2. **Determine what you're willing to give in exchange** for this money and effort. This is often a missed step for many people. Be clear on the value you will offer, what you're willing to give up, and the tenacity you're committed to in

building it. Focus on what value you are creating in exchange for the money to flow into your life.

3. **Establish a clear timeline** for when you wish to achieve this goal.

4. **Outline the exact steps you need to take** to bring this into reality. Consider what would make it more likely to become real. The key here is to get realistic about what you can achieve.

5. **Write a clear statement of intention** with the exact steps. Specify how much money you intend to receive, what you're giving and committing to in exchange, and the daily steps you need to take to make it a reality. Consistency, discipline, and habits are crucial here, as they will help you prioritize your time and energy effectively.

6. **Write your ultimate goal**—with timelines and specifics—on a sticky note (or somewhere visible) and read it to yourself every morning and night. Commit to this plan and activate daily discipline to make it your reality.

If you follow these steps, you will create a roadmap of action for yourself. You need to move in alignment with your intention every day, deeply believing that it will happen even if there's no immediate evidence. These small steps and reverse engineering will help break your goal into smaller, more achievable steps, increasing the likelihood of success.

Consider hiring a coach or someone who's already done it. This has been one of the keys to my success. Anytime I wanted to pivot, hiring a coach or being in close proximity to someone who has already achieved what I desired was crucial. This will not only keep you on track with action but can potentially expedite the process.

At times, we deeply desire action but lack the motivation to stay on course with tenacity and discipline. In this case, telling others about your plans can help you stay on track. There's something powerful about broadcasting your intentions to trusted people that keeps you committed to your course of action. Choose a few trusted people in your life who will cheerlead you along the way. This approach recognizes that taking action isn't just about motivation or inspiration but also about mindset shifts. You could also find an accountability buddy—someone you can check in with regularly to ensure you don't let yourself off the hook for not getting important tasks done. Intentionally creating an environment of accountability can help you feel supported as you rise.

As you navigate your journey of action, there will inevitably be moments of failure. But seeing these moments as opportunities for rapid experimentation is key. Learn from failure and view setbacks as essential components of growth rather than obstacles. Choose what works for you and leave the rest. Giving yourself the grace to experiment is crucial during this action phase. It also helps you overcome self-doubt and allows you to see failure as learning rather than a reflection of your abilities.

Taking an action-oriented approach to your goals helps demystify the act of movement, showing that with the right strategies and mindset, anyone can turn their ideas into reality. Everything hard in life is really just a series of small, easy steps. Wealth is no different for women. We often believe it's impossible to get from where we are today to where we want to go. But when we break it down into small pieces and explore the possibility that it's achievable—whether it's paying off debt, building wealth, learning more, or stepping into a new paradigm of generational wealth—the sum of the parts leads to a newly manifested life. This is how I went from $50,000 in debt as a single mom to a happily remarried mother of three and a joyful, free multi-millionaire. It was belief, energetics, education, getting in the right rooms, and, above all, taking action.

Now, you might be wondering about those two houses I added to my portfolio during maternity leave with my son. Did they work out, or were they actually money pits?

Well, they worked out better than I could have ever planned. My focus at the time was to provide great homes for tenants while securing a new source of income to secure my children's future. Despite feeling sick during the purchase process, these little houses have delivered incredible returns. In less than three years, not only have our tenants collectively paid down about $30,000 of the mortgage, but we've also seen a 200% return in less than two years. This is mind-blowing. I never could have imagined it would turn out this well, especially with a house that smelled like cat pee. Most importantly, this has contributed to my family's incredible financial security. Now, we don't have to worry about whether we can afford the school we want for our children or the holiday we desire. We have the freedom of choice to practice discernment and lifestyle alignment the way we choose. And this is available for you, too—this incredible sense of freedom.

The funny thing about money is the more you have, the less it becomes about money. Rather, it becomes more about helping others, higher purpose, consciousness, and internal riches of how you want to live your life. It really becomes about how you—the gorgeous, infinite, beautiful woman you are—want to live this amazing 1 in 4 billion chance of life that she was gifted. To maximize her true wealth and abundance in freedom with her time and to transcend the white picket fence—her way.

CONTEMPLATION QUESTIONS

Okay! We have finally arrived. The last chapter and last set of contemplation questions. What a journey we have been on together. Thank you for committing to the embodiment of this book. By actioning and embodying the learnings, you shift yourself from being a consumer of content into a creator of your wealthiest life! A few last ones for the road:

1. Do I tend to focus on action or perfection? Why?

_____

_____

_____

_____

2. How can I shift into action in my life? Consider small steps you could take on a daily basis to bring forth your desires.

_____

_____

_____

_____

3. What area am I most afraid to step into as I rise to the wealthiest version of myself? What about it is most scary to me? Why?

_____

_____

_____

_____

4. What is my most common response to feeling my nervous system activate in the face of taking action? (Think fight, flight, fawn, or freeze responses.)

a. _____ Asserting dominance

b. _____ Urgency to solve or fix what is at hand

c. _____ Overthinking before I move

d. _____ Procrastinating

e. _____ Constantly seeking validation or reassurance

5. Now that I am aware of my typical response, how can I work toward quicker action next time I see this come up?

_____

_____

_____

_____

6. If we know that action is a muscle and a gateway to overcome nerves, what is one thing you could do to step into that decision that makes you most afraid? What is it? When can you do it? How can I keep myself accountable for this?

_____

_____

_____

_____

ACTIVATIONS

1. Consider the one big wealth goal you have at the moment. Reverse engineer this with realism on how you can bring it to life using the following six-step process:
   a. Clearly define the goal you have in mind as it relates to your wealth, abundance, and freedom. You need to be as specific as possible here—generalizations will not work.
   b. Determine what you are willing to give in return for the exchange of this money and effort. Be clear on the value you will offer, as well as what you are willing to give up and the tenacity you are committed to in building it. The focus is what value are you creating in exchange for this money to flow into your life.
   c. Establish a clear timeline in which you wish to achieve the goal you have described.
   d. Now, figure out what exact steps you need to take to bring this into your reality. Consider what would make it more likely for this to be real. The key here is to get realistic about what you can achieve.
   e. Write a clear statement of intention with the exact steps associated with it. These daily steps are where consistency, discipline, and habits come in. Get crystal clear on what you need to do every single day to make it happen.

    f. Write your ultimate goal with timelines and specifics on a sticky note (or somewhere you can see it often), and read it to yourself every morning and every night before bed. Decide that you will commit to this plan and activate daily discipline to make it your reality.

2. Now, go *do* the damn thing!

Conclusion

After writing this book, I have come to the conclusion that writing a book is an absolute labor of love. It is your innermost thoughts poured out on paper over hundreds of coffees, quiet contemplations, and meaningful reflections. But in the end, the journey of writing has led me to realize that true wealth—our highest sense of it—is about falling in love with our lives. Falling so deeply in love with your life means that money simply becomes the paint on this beautiful canvas we call life.

As a wealth and empowerment coach who now helps women become the joyful first millionaires in their families, I often make people feel uncomfortable by talking about money so much. As a woman, people often project the idea that talking about money means it's all I care about. After reading this book, I hope you now know that the very opposite is true. The more money you have, the less it becomes about the money. Instead, as a sisterhood of women, it becomes about empowering other women to do the same. It's about cheering other women on as they achieve radical success. It's about shifting a paradigm and getting more money into the hands of conscious women around the world. Together, we can do so much good.

My call to you is to truly fall in love with your life again: to understand deeply that money is simply an outer manifestation of who we are and the value we create in this world, how we feel, and the frequency we emit. And don't wait for the money to come. You decide to be happy, you do the inner work first, you deeply know what brings you joy, and then the money becomes the outer manifestation. It becomes the tool to go and do more—to paint and design this beautiful, wealthy, abundant, free life.

I want you to know deep in your soul that this journey we call life is worth it. It's worth taking the risk, expanding beyond your comfort zone, and knowing that your deepest desires are hints of what you should be doing with your time. That all of your desires and life alignment are within your reach, all within the quantum of potentiality for you, waiting for you to grab. Be brave enough to transcend the white picket fence and grasp true wealth, happiness, joy, and financial freedom in this lifetime. That is my wish for you: to go first and shift not just your world but to become an example for women for generations to come.

Thank you from the bottom of my heart. By purchasing and reading this book, you have helped make my dream of empowering women around the world to become joyful, first-generation millionaires a reality. I hope that my words and experiences have lit the way forward for you to become the wealthiest version of yourself in a way that is joyful and aligned. This book is just the tip of the iceberg. The potential that lies within you is infinite. I hope you know that any dream you have within your soul is in the realm of possibility and that money will no longer be the thing that holds you back.

If you would like to explore the ideas explained in this book further, I invite you to visit my website, where you can find many resources to help quantum leap your wealth. You can find everything at www.quantumfemwealth.com. I offer private one-on-one coaching sessions, group coaching programs, and courses. There are free tools available, including a net worth calculator, a free money blocks download, and even a free lifestyle alignment exercise. You can join my email list or my Facebook group if you just want to get in the room. I would be deeply honored to have you.

Now that you've reached the end of this book, I hope not only that you have some great new ideas on the energetics of wealth but also that you feel activated and ready to take action on the deepest desires of your heart. I encourage you to go back, embody the ideas, do the activations, and practice the steps. I want you to know beyond a shadow of a doubt that your deepest desires of wealth, freedom, and happiness are available to you too. You get to choose your "all," design your life, and have wealth beyond your wildest imagination. You get to write the rules of your life and transcend the typical white picket fence into ultimate aligned wealth, abundance, and freedom.

Thank You For Reading My Book!

READY TO EMBRACE MORE WEALTH IN YOUR LIFE?

Just to say thanks for buying and reading my book, I would like to offer you a FREE 30-minute session with the Quantum Femme Wealth Team to explore our courses, classes, and resources! You can chat about anything money-related and explore programs that might be a fit if you are READY to take your wealth to new heights!

To Book Now, Scan the QR Code:

I appreciate your interest in my book and value your feedback as it helps me improve future versions of this book. I would appreciate it if you could leave your invaluable review on Amazon.com with your feedback. Thank you!

www.ingramcontent.com/pod-product-compliance
Lightning Source LLC
Chambersburg PA
CBHW031503180326
41458CB00044B/6681/J